MW01596085

"I'm Home!"

a Dog's Never Ending Love Story

Brent Atwater

True Stories from Around the World
Plus a Q & A Pet Reincarnation & Animal Communication Chapter

Library of Congress Cataloging-in-Publication Data

Paperback ISBN: 9781439211861
Hardcover ISBN: 9781439267813
EBook ISBN:
Kindle: ASIN: B003UNK0MC
Audio:

1st printing: 2010 USA
Canada
UK, AU, SA check with distributor
Publisher's Price Higher in Other Countries
**Animals/Pet / Lifestyles / Self-Help / Spiritual Growth / Inspirational / Pet Loss/ Pet Grief
Support / Body, Mind & Spirit / Reincarnation / Spirituality / Family & Relationships / Death /
Grief / Bereavement / Self Development / Healing / Nonfiction / Animals / Pets/ Pets / Dogs /
General/ Dogs / Pets / Animal Stories/ Pet Heaven/ Audio Books / eBooks**

Please visit Brent Atwater's Web site at:
www.BrentAtwater.com
www.JustPlainLoveBooks.com

This *Just Plain Love®* *Book*
is given to YOU

To: _____

Message: _____

_____

Date: _____

with
LOTS of LOVE and KISSES!!!

From: _____

and

Friend

Acknowledgements

I want to thank you the reader for taking the time to explore my *Just Plain Love*® Books and for allowing me to share what I have learned and am learning about pet past lives and animal reincarnation and animal communication through my and other individuals personal experiences.

Special thanks to Michael Wellford and my precious fur, finned and feathered companions for their contributions and enduring patience with me and my spiritual path.

and to

Tracy Heinlein owner of Blastoff Border Collies in Westville Oklahoma, whose B24 Sage and FA Blastoff Simmer are the wonderful parents of Blastoff's My Best Friend.

It is my intent and hope that this information will facilitate inspiration, greater perspectives, and expanded awareness in your life.

I thank those who have supported and encouraged my journey and the authors, speakers and teachers who contributed to shaping my consciousness.

My gratitude also goes to:

Special thanks to the NC State Veterinary School ICU earth angels for watching over Friend, and to Dr. Keith Harrison, Vicki, "Aunt Susan" and Jessica for taking care of and looking after all my "children." Many thanks to Bonnie Buchanan of Bon-Clyde Learning Center for Professional Canines for Friend's certification as a Canine Good Citizen (CGC) and Therapy Dog (TDI)!

and to

Each individual who shared their story in this book so that our readers can derive hope and be inspired by "all that is."

Dedication

This is written to honor my entire inspiring and beloved canine,
feline, equine and other animal teachers, guardians and
companions with whom I shared my experiences,
learning and life.
From my heart to yours, thank you!
To Thomas Michael Ramseur Wellford,
whose life, love, and passing made my understanding possible.
I shall always hold you and hear you in my heart,
my soul, and my dreams.
To those very special people and fur babies who have been my
joy, and with whom I have shared and share hope, laughter
and LIFE!!!

TABLE OF CONTENTS

Brent Atwater's *Just Plain Love® Books* presents

INTRODUCTION

If you are reading this introduction you're probably an animal lover or someone you know needs a GREAT BIG HUG! If you just plain love® animals or have experienced the loss of a beloved furry, feathered or finned soul mate, have an interest in pet past lives, pet reincarnation, animal communication or care about another individual who is grieving over the loss of their much loved animal companion, this is THE book you're looking for!

The "I'm Home!" book series (Dogs, Cats and Horses) shares heartwarming pet and animal stories that illustrate the various signs and different events that occurred during the times when my clients, friends, family and myself suffered through pet loss, grieving, beginning the new search process and how each of us was led to be reunited with our beloved reincarnated animal companions. PLUS, there is a special section that has questions and answers about the pet reincarnation process, prayers for reincarnation confirmation, how to recognize your pet and animal communication with them.

I offer Friend's past lives and pet reincarnation story from my heart and from my soul's "experiences" during each of my beloved pets' sickness, degenerating health, disease, chronic illness and even sudden or inevitable death to crossing over the Rainbow Bridge. I have been the "Mother," caregiver, playmate, instructor, cheerleader, medical intuitive, pet psychic, animal and interspecies communicator, energy healer, medical consultant, and bearer of good and bad tidings. I have supported my client's beloved animal companions who were dying and helped in their transition. I have shared disorders, despair, untimely death, miracles, healing and triumphant joy personally with my "fur children," and with my client's pets and animal partners.

Many thanks to all God's wonderful and cherished creatures who have taught me what I share with you in this book that I write to honor all their lives.

Although this book chronicles Friend's story, it's not really about Friend per se. His reincarnations are the embodiment of the lessons as I learned them and how my heart's awareness grew with each death and rebirth, and how my mind expanded its awareness with new found realities each past life and new incarnation presented.

Editing this book was excruciatingly painful for me, as I relived each story inside my heart when checking the formatting, spelling et al. I hope that each story gives strength to your heart and supports what you are going though after the loss of your pet.

It is my intent that this book warms your heart, comforts, reassures and helps inspire hope in addition to providing insight that expands your awareness of all things possible and real! I hope the true stores give you tingles and goose bumps (a friend calls them God bumps) of confirmation, and that you can relate to the thoughts, feeling and experiences of each owner and perhaps think.   Hummmmmm, that's related to what's going on in my life…….. since my pet died.

As a holistic integrative energy medicine specialist, throughout the years in my practice as a medical intuitive diagnostician, intuitive healthcare consultant, distant energy healer and a pet reincarnation expert, I have gathered the results, stories and testimonials from clients, friends and family members, (in addition to my personal experiences), that concluded we all experienced profound healing and expanded awareness when we recognized that our beloved animal companions reincarnated to be with us again. Our fur, finned or feathered family always adds to and enhances the quality and quantity of our life.

Enjoy!

You're invited to submit your pet's or animal's reincarnation stories to:

Brent Atwater
Just Plain Love® Books - Pet Stories

Email:
Brent@BrentAtwater.com
Friend@JustPlainLoveBooks.com

My dog died!

I was DEVASTED!!!

He was the love of my life!

My heart experienced gut wrenching pain

and

agonizing loneliness.

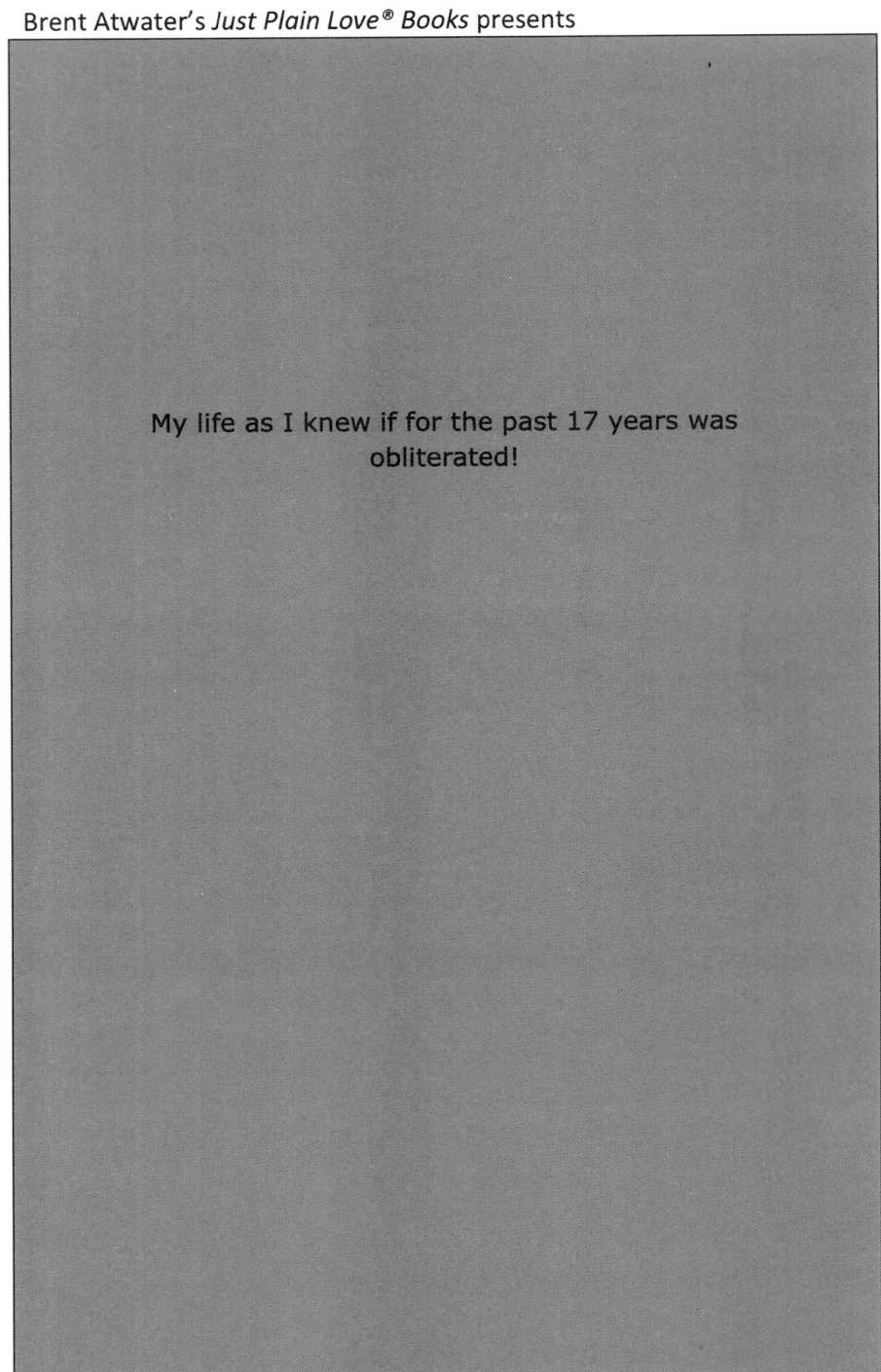

My life as I knew if for the past 17 years was obliterated!

Being in an empty house was more than I could bear!

For months afterwards before bedtime

I would stand numb at the outside door

like I had done for years at "potty time."

Nights were horrifically quiet!

The emptiness and darkness was traumatizing.

I couldn't bear to put up his photos, food bowls or toys……..
What do I do with his collar and leash?

Today,
when I looked into that puppy's eyes,
there was something very familiar.
Something my heart and soul responded to
and recognized.

Something about that tiny furry fluff felt familiar.

Perhaps it was the way he looked at me,
as if he had done it many times before...

Surely I thought,
not again?!

With all my heart,

I prayed for it to be so!

My first dog Sunday was named for the day we got her. She was the little bitty beige one that wiggled out of the clustered puppies to adopt me.

She was so tiny that I had to cradle her in my arms to protect her on our ride home.

23

She was my beloved companion through childhood and adolescence. We slept like cuddled littermates and grew up together. Who knew that wet puppy kisses from over a shoulder and toe fur in your face in the morning would be adorable, or that playing tug of war to get the best position under the bedspread would become a nightly ritual after our "treat?"

Although Sunday Dog was not a service or assistance dog, we established a bond and familiar patterns that wove our lives together. We developed routines, habits and special games just she and I knew. Do car windows come without nose prints or furniture and clothes without "love fur" keepsakes? Not in our home!

24

Sunday taught me how to play. She taught me kindness, patience and tolerance. With her steadfast big brown eyes she taught me that temper tantrums and yelling are unacceptable, and that all encompassing loving hugs and understanding solve everything.

Every day when I walked home from elementary school, there was Sunday sitting on the side of the street in front of our house patiently awaiting my arrival. One day a car accidentally ran over her. She still managed to be there with a crushed foreleg, multiple cuts and bruises holding on until I came home. She always followed my bike to the ice cream parlor and enjoyed her share while sitting on the steps beside me. Many times, I would get Sunday her own cone! She liked vanilla best! One of her favorite things was to ride in the back of my Dad's boat to ensure that I was protected while we were skiing and swimming

25

· SEP · 59

Sunday's friendship sustained and comforted me through life's emotional traumas and teenage boyfriends,
as she listened with a cocked head and understanding pricked ear.

She was never more than a heartbeat away.

Her watchful loving eyes guarded over my being and no one was admitted to our world without her consent

.

We sang and danced together to celebrate what I considered triumphs.

When I was happy she was. When I was sad, she would lie very quiet and still and look into the depths of my soul with her heartfelt protective gaze.

Sometimes she'd put a cold nose in my lap or a single paw on me just to let me know that she was there for me.

On the day I graduated from High School, she suddenly,
unexplainably collapsed in our driveway.
The veterinarian diagnosed advanced colon cancer and felt
it was in her best interest to be euthanized.
She meant the world to me.
My soul had to be there for and with her, as she had been
for me.

I gathered her favorite "bankie and boo boos," and carefully,
lovingly and tenderly placed her with them.

I held her in my arms as her trusting eyes focused on
my face.   She listened to my heart's song while she tolerated
the injection that sent her to heaven.

My heart died when hers stopped beating.

27

Years passed.

I couldn't find and was devoid of any unconditional connection
like the one that I had with my Sunday Dog
who did not know she wasn't a "person," probably why my
relationship's breakup was easier than I imagined.

I was soul lonely.

I didn't know what an animal or interspecies communicator
was, but I kept seeing her alive and well in my dreams.
Sometimes she was represented in another dog form
and didn't look like herself,
but I inherently knew it was her.

I could feel her with me.

Two more years passed
while I searched myriad litters of puppies to no avail.

My heart ached.
I felt my life though busy, was hollow.

Out of the blue,
from the hundreds of ads that I had half heartedly read
since she died,
a particular newspaper classified caught my eye.

I drove to the house that Sunday afternoon
preparing to be disappointed again.

It's not that the puppies I interviewed weren't cute or smart,
I just knew that unexplainable
"something"
was missing!

I played with the fat male that waddled toward me
and scooped up several others
while constantly shoving, pushing away and stepping over
the annoying little runt that determinedly
sat by my ankle no matter what I was doing
as if I was "her person."

I took my time making my decision.
When I notified the owner which pup I wanted,
he informed me that the only one left was the runt.
I was determined to go home with a dog.

I begrudgingly paid for the scruffie ivory colored fur ball
that the Universe had dealt,
I thought,
to my slow choice making.

When I reluctantly and finally picked her up to examine what I paid for, her eyes talked to me in a way that resonated to my soul's core.

I felt a sense of "home" return to our household again.

Electra more rapidly than normal joined my daily routine as if it were old times and she had been there before.
How could this be I thought?
My heart sang again.

She participated in and over French fries, in helping me make
all my major life decisions.
She was wise beyond her years, understood everything
we talked about and knew how to handle every life event.
Electra stabilized my life and kept me sane
uring my most trying times!

We went through a divorce; several job related moves,
heartworm treatments and life's numerous ups and downs.
She never left my side.

Even if I was floating in the chair at the lake,
she would swim out to join me.

Electra took care of, protected and watched over everyone!

Electra was my second skin, my shadow, my "child."
We were connected by our very breath, telepathic thought,
heartbeat and soul. She set the standard for all to follow:
thoughtful, wise, kind, gentle, playful, SMART!
and would have given her life to save mine.
As her time was nearing, I would often see her silhouetted
against the terrace doors staring outside, as if she was
memorizing her earthly surroundings.

When she died in her sleep of old age,
a part of me died with her.
I awoke bolt upright in the middle of the night
inherently knowing she had crossed the Rainbow Bridge.

Everything inside of me against all common sense,
felt she would never leave me and that we would be reunited.

Though her body left, I ran with her spirit in my mind and
could feel her on my bed at night just before I went to sleep.

Often I saw her out of the corner of my eye
or felt her as a cool tingly nudge on my hand.
I told no one! I knew I was not crazy.

35

My friends thought I was misguided
and had "lost it"
when I was intent on finding a dog
"that had Electra's energy."

They were unaware of animal reincarnation and thought
I was being absurd about the fact that Electra's spirit might
return like I had read that humans do.

When I considered consulting a pet psychic,
that idea brought responses from my friends like
"what are you thinking, have you lost your mind?"

I just kept praying, hoping and

searching…………..

There were other wonderful dogs that shared life with me
between reincarnations.
It was different looking into their eyes,
you didn't experience that special soul connection
that you "know" in your gut with your reincarnated pet.
My "love bug" "handsome fella," the "Boo Bear," "smart as can
be" cute little Polka Dot, the Tweedle Dee and Tweedle Dum
sisters, Orestes, loving "kind hearted" Blessing or elegant and
picky Noysekophf and KT were all <u>very</u> special to me.
I deeply love them all!
We shared many heartfelt memories; like finding a SOAKING
WET tennis ball as a "gift" on my pillow one night.

Seven years later at a most inopportune time,
my soul was relentless in creating a craving for a puppy.
I made a few bogus calls to placate my inner persistence.
A few nights later about 6:30 a message on my answering
machine stated: "I heard you wanted a red and white
Border collie puppy. We had a litter of six, unbeknownst to us
the Mother dog took them outside and five of them froze.
If you want the one that survived,
I'll sell him cheap since he has good bloodlines, but he may be
brain damaged." Everything inside me said bad circumstances
and go get that puppy!

At 10:30 pm on a Sunday night in 8 inches of snow
in a MacDonald's parking lot, 5 week old "Friend" became mine.

38

When I looked into Friend's eyes, I just "knew" we had been together before. We bonded instantaneously! His training was incredibly easy.

At 6 weeks of age he almost immediately did everything my other dogs had done, including their quirky special loveable habits like "discussing" everything. He put up with my "I love you, yes I do" songs and baby talk, and made noises back to me.

From 8 weeks on, he understood all my moods and hardly ever missed the meaning of what I was communicating.
He was quite the "talker" and "singer" too. We were a duet that would make you laugh. We had a great Christmas routine!

We communicated with each other with our eyes.
From the beginning, this puppy knew exactly where the toys
that I had saved were kept, and he slept in the same position in
the same bed spot as my other soul dogs had done.

For 17.5 years Friend was my "baby dog," guardian, playmate,
best friend, co-worker, partner, confidant and teacher.
We were inseparable. He was the love of my life! He was my
everything! He activated my spiritual side and taught me about
a soul's contract (that I actually had one).
At 15.5 he slipped on a slick floor while rounding a corner,
fell and became paralyzed.
The veterinarian advised euthanasia stating
"he had lived a good long life."

I was NOT ready to let him go!

I inherently KNEW he was not ready to go!

After many many long soul bearing, begging and pleading talks
with God and even more heartfelt tearful prayers,
Friend's plight activated my abilities as a medical intuitive and
medical intuitive diagnostician.
I could look at him and see inside his body.
I could see his broken vertebrae, and see where his spinal cord
nerves were damaged. I knew about his nose infection and
his diminished lung function before the doctor would tell me.
It was a frightening awakening of my gifts,
yet Friend had chosen to experience this entire ordeal
in order to be my spiritual teacher.

Friend's medical predicament induced me to search, research,
and to eventually believe and trust in holistic, integrative
and alternative therapies
of energy medicine and energy healing.
His "accident" expanded my awareness beyond
current traditional medical limitations and mindsets.
The doctors told me Friend would never walk again.
My soul knew otherwise!

He was the first dog ever to be released from the NC State University School of Veterinary Medicine hospital on a breathing machine because his oxygen values were approximately 55. Due to his fall, Friend would never breathe on his own.

I prayed for guidance to know how to heal him.

I worked with him for months, praying, being guided and learning how to heal him.

120 days after his accident, Friend walked into the veterinarian school's hospital on his own and with no oxygen assistance for his last check up.

His vertebrae, discs and spinal cord nerves were restored and regenerated by the healing energy
that his accident had activated within me.
His oxygen blood levels were now within normal range.

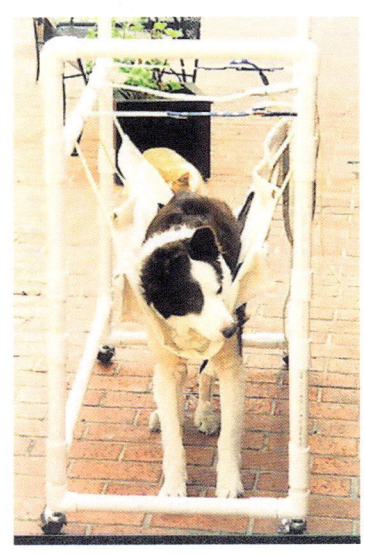

Even though all of Friend's healing results were documented
by X-rays, blood work and pulmonary test results,
his final release report stated at the bottom
"We don't know what you did, but keep it up.
We wish Friend all the best."

Friend walked and had a wonderful quality of life for 2 more
years.

Thanks to Friend's journey,
my new life as a medical intuitive and energy healer began.
I honor and celebrate all of his contributions to my life and for
all the things that he taught me for the benefit of others.

God bless my spiritual guide and master teacher Friend!

When my human soul mate/twin flame was unexpectedly and
suddenly killed in a car crash,
Friend was there to console me and "talk" about everything.
I buried my tears in his luxurious ruff.
He is a part of my life journey and always and forever etched
and ingrained into my heart, soul and a part of my being.
He taught me to know reincarnation with a soul pet is reality.

As Friend drew his last breath resulting from kidney failure,
staring into my eyes, I knew that his soul would return.
Even during my greatest anguish,
for the first time my heart understood patience.
I knew that I would "know" when he replaced his old
and ill body with a new one in order to come home to me.

I chose Electra as a companion for Friend while he was aging.
She eagerly bounced in and out of our lives with hugs, kisses,
wet tennis balls, wiggling unbridled curiosity
and endless "wide open" energy for nonstop walks.

They always slept together,
and seeing them sleep on their backs with feet nonchalantly
and indiscriminately splayed wide open to expose tummies to
the warm sun, was one of my favorite memoires!

Everyone said "there's something 'special' about that dog."
I knew why,
when she sang her "woo woo" song to greet people,
she was my precious little "squirrel girl," "Miss Personality!"
Every morning we would choose THE perfect bandana
from her extensive collection
of multiple styles and color choices.
Some days required several wardrobe changes
to suit each special occasion.

Electra was stunned and scared the day she and Mikey sniffed his cold body; it was as if she sensed that Friend had passed the torch for her to take care of "Mommy."
The old dog had trained her well.
I now understood the difference between a soul connected dog like Friend was, and a wonderful pet like Electra.

It was a transformative experience for me when months later Friend's spirit "walked in" to Electra's life form. He taught me about another level of consciousness that I had not known throughout his previous incarnations.

Friend showed me that a soul, who had previously died,
can "walk into" an existing body, a concept that I had never
even considered before that time.

Electra not only maintained her own personal qualities,
she now embodied and exhibited the added personality,
behavior traits and preferences of Friend.
Their two spirits had combined in Electra's body!

We bonded and engaged in a level of closeness and positive
interdependence that I had not known before. She knew my
next move before I did! We read each other's minds,
yet we always discovered wonderful new surprises
to share between us.

She was a happy very intense little girl and her smile made my
heart smile. I felt safe, special, comforted and loved in her
presence. Her joy and eagerness to experience each day
with a renewed curiosity was infectious and uplifting.
She taught me to reappreciate lots of things
that had become mundane in my life.

51

As she grew older, sometimes after "work" we would sit in front
of my computer and preview puppy sites for hours.
She would stand with her paws on the desk and look intently
at the computer screen so I could get her approval on which
sites had the best red and white Border collie litters.
Instinctively and sadly I knew we were practicing for a future
event. I promised Electra that when it was time,
I would choose from the site that she was most attentive to
in our searches.

Our relationship embraced 13 wonderful magical years until
mammary cancer took her gorgeous mahogany body.
Her spirit did not want to leave me;
I ached for her not to depart.

Although she fought hard, her body was beyond staying.
I honored that horrible and painful fact.

Whenever I leave my dogs, I have always put on my reddest
lipstick and kissed them on the forehead,

to symbolize my love always surrounding and protecting them.
while we were apart.

As she left,

I knew her energy would return
because she would not say goodbye.

She was still taking care of me
when her eyes permanently closed.

Once again my soul shattered!

God, how I miss her!

I still cry for her in my heart…..

53

For years after Friend's and Electra's passing,
I'd find a memory filled toy or
hear familiar sounds in another room. At times, my cats
seemed to be paying attention to an imaginary "friend."
I continually consoled myself during my depression and crying
bouts by watching "our" favorite website's puppy images.

Each loss of my soul pet had gotten more painful.
It seemed that the older I became, the worse the pain was.
When I would force myself forward to procure a puppy,
each time that I would call about the one I picked,
it had just been sold.
One exasperated breeder that I had contacted too late too
many times, stated, "perhaps you should send a deposit"
to which I responded,
"When its time I'll know."

I watched endless months
that turned to even more years
of weekly photos, daily puppy updates,
videos and rescue webcams.

Nothing!

I really didn't even care because my heart still mourned to my
core.   I also didn't want to feel hurt this bad again.

However, I kept being compelled
to continue watching puppy updates
and checking all the sites and shelters
no matter how upset they made me.

Then, one day while watching Electra's favorite site,
this fluffy little red and white fur ball in motion,
dragging a LARGE stuffed toy in his mouth
ran gleefully zoom-zoom-zoom across my computer screen.

My heart unexpectedly started pounding,
my stomach squenched up
and tears welled up in my eyes.

I frantically bookmarked the video.

I must have watched, rewatched, cried and rewatched and
memorized that video hundreds of times!!!

I could feel that puppy in my soul!

I called the owner to check his status. He was available albeit 2500 miles away. I thought, "3.5 hours on a plane, TOO far to fly the little fellow with stopovers."

Who knows why, but I was compelled to call a second time to recheck the flight schedules. Unbeknownst to me the Universe had arranged for the airline carrier to add an extra holiday nonstop flight from the Midwest area to our airport.

Now I had no excuses not to get him!
I had been unencumbered for years and a new pup,
well…………………
I talked to and questioned the puppy's guardian till she was probably really tired of me.   In one conversation, she jokingly referred to him as "bad boy." I asked why.

She stated that he had a fabulous personality, was "quite the talker" and had, "a strange white marking on his right hip." She said she would send me more of his newborn photos and other pictures so I could see the unusual white marking.

The image took my breath away and sent chills up my spine
and all my friends into a chorus of "what don't you get?"
This pup had already been assigned to me by a higher level
than any of us knew at that time. It was as if
God commissioned an Angel to paint
a monogram of my signature on this puppy's hip
so I would **clearly** understand
that he was meant to be mine!

With a weary heart, afraid and excited I met him at the airport,
VERY apprehensive!
I had never picked an unhugged puppy before
from just photos and videos, much less from a distance.
What if I had the wrong pup and we didn't connect?

I carefully tiptoed up to the huge beige crate so I wouldn't startle the tiny reddish brown puppy huddled in a corner inside. When I unlatched the door, he launched out of that crate and immediately sat all 7 pounds of 9 weeks old mahogany fluff right down in front of me. He looked up and stared directly into my eyes as if to say "where have you been?
Now let's get on with our life!"

I knew his name would be "My Best Friend"
Then he scrambled onto my lap. That warm new puppy smell filled the car while he slept in the fold of my arm all the way to my house that had now become our home.

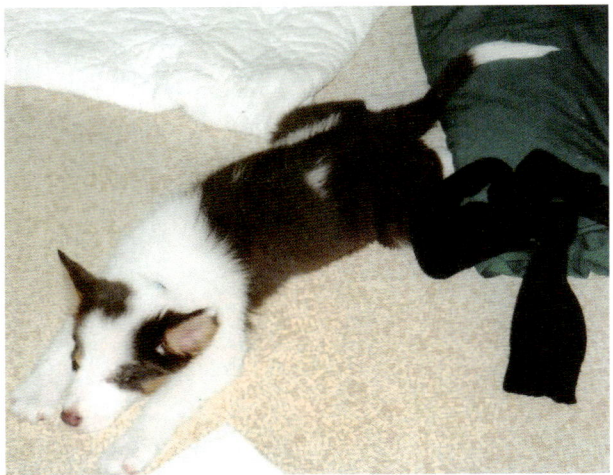

He responded to his "old" name without missing a beat. He
<u>knew</u> where his bed was, recognized his past life toys and
regathered them into his same toy spot where they were
supposed to be! He did not even inspect the new toys,
he wanted HIS toys! He talks, carries on great discussions,
sings, and does all the things all my other soul dogs "did."

When I look into his eyes we never left one another.
He is my "baby dog," my forever best Friend.

When my heart asked where you have been, his spirit replied:
I had to exchange my old body for this new one
so I could be in your life again.

At 10 weeks old with one perfect white tipped pricked ear
and a random VERY creative expressive one,
Friend knew and responded to my old dog's commands.
No major training was necessary, just "reminders."
And can he ever work those blue and gold eyes and his gold
"cheekies" subtly to get almost anything he wants!

Wherever I am, he is!
He jumps right in or wedges his pink brown nose into EVERY
thing to investigate or participate in what I'm doing!

New Friend "back talks" and "discusses" many directives that I
give. If he doesn't like something, he has a vast repertoire of
"talking" sounds to let me know he is NOT happy
with my command or what is going on.
We've discussed and STILL discuss "stay" or "no" MANY times!

His rendition of Electra's "woo woo" song is a hoot! He even
has ME trained to fetch his ball from under the furniture
or out of the pond!

He's my old adult dog with few puppy moments except he
moves at "full throttle - wide open," and is learning how to
operate this body's new feet.

You can tell he's awake because he's chewing!
Can "tuggies," "chewies," smelly toys, soggy balls and
"Mr. Bears" strewn ALL OVER my once clean house, and
incessant, I mean INCESSANT squeaky toys be truly adorable?
When he's quiet, I worry!

Even Mikey our senior cat recognizes this 90 day reincarnate.
She lived w th first Friend and Electra.
She slept on first Friend's grave for the longest time.

It was like a class reunion.
Mikey knew they knew each other from before,
but they didn't know how to act now.
Mikey instigated head bumps, a game of tag with a
playful paw bat, and she nonchalantly weaves back and fo-th
under Friend's stomach before eating dinner together and
then cleaning his face and ears.

They can be seen intertwined in the late afternoon sun napping,
or haggling for space on my bed's pillow each night.
She settles more and more easily into second place as he
grows. Sometimes Mikey exasperated by "His Puppyhood," has
to "explain it" with a swipe of her claw to
inspire respect for his feline buddy.

When Friend does a major "no no," (like teething on an antique or marking new territory), I'm momentarily willing to give him away free to anyone who would take him.

Then he slinks down the hall tail tucked between his legs with that B illuminated brightly against his mahogany fur, and my heart melts.

I even made a little song that I sing to "His Puppyhood" when he has been V E R Y naughty to help me get over his "mistakes":
"When I'm in doubt
and want to throw you out,
I can clearly seeeeeeeeeeeeeeee
With that big bright white B,
God made you 'specially for me! ☺"

I feel blessed to have gentle paw
pads stroking my face
to awaken me each morning.
We share lots of bonding hugs.
He's a "love machine!" and
demands to be the center of
attention (of course!)

Eventually Friend prods me with
his cold wet nose, smelling of
warm puppy breath
insisting with very intense eyes,
that I need to get up
and feed him now!

Then he jumps off "our" bed and stands there barking
until I comply!

Each day as we grow older together,
I'm continuously reminded that all the eccentric little habits,
routines, traits, favorite toys, foods, spots and tricks
known only to my soul and my "Sunday dogs,"
is back home with me
in a non returnable "monogrammed" fur form
named Friend!

Questions and Answers about
Pet Past Lives, Animal Reincarnation
& Animal Communication

When you've lost your beloved pet, service dog, companion animal, assistance dog, therapy pet, soul pet partner and forever finned, feathered or fur baby, - love of your life, "child," don't lose hope. Listen to your heart's urgings, watch your dreams, and follow your soul's knowing. Pay attention to your intuition and inner guidance.

If you feel that you want to or must hold onto your pet's beds, belongings and toys, there is a reason. Some part of your soul's inner being knows that they will be back.

Each and every animal's soul is a spirit composed of eternal energy that lives forever in our vast Universe. Whether or not it's your soul pet, forever fur baby, animal spirit guide or spiritual teacher in an animal form, God/ the Universe honors his choice to reincarnate or "walk in" to be with you in various physical bodies throughout your life time.

It's not just about your pet's soul's path or singular lessons, your pet's reincarnation, "walk in" or "over soul" is about what you have to accomplish **together**. He/she will continue to reincarnate, "walk in," "soul braid" or "over soul" until your combined learning opportunities are complete.

 Know that your pet is never gone forever; he's just changed the form of his life force energy. Give their spirit time to generate a new body if they choose to return.
Your heart will know when it's time to look for them again. When you reunite with them, your souls will instantly recognize each other and understand "I'm Home!"

Basic concepts of Reincarnation:
  Some individuals, who have not experienced the real life opportunity and true knowing of a reincarnated pet, feel that pets do not return either because they have no need to or they don't have lessons to learn. Others who have not experienced an angel animal that reincarnates suggest that a loved one who passed may have sent you a special furry, finned or feathered baby to be with you. In my experience, animals reincarnate for diverse reasons.

A soul connected forever pet is usually a spiritual teacher, guide or guardian spirit that travels with you in pet form throughout your earthly journey.

Reincarnation is the belief that when one's physical body dies, their spirit is able to choose to be reborn into another body because the energy known as the spirit or soul is everlasting. Not all people believe in reincarnation; however it's interesting that most people agree that you will be with all your pets that have gone to the Rainbow Bridge when your body dies and crosses to the other side.

Reincarnation is a concept that is a universally held belief especially among the older larger religions. Therefore to me, it is a reasonable expectation that many people would believe their pets will reincarnate.

FYI, in 2007 a respected British leading independent research company YouGov conducted a study and found that dogs proved to be the type of animal most likely to be considered a reincarnation by pet owners: 51% said they had or have dogs in which they believe to be a re-incarnation while 44% said it was a cat.

The reincarnation information below was gathered from friends, clients and my personal experiences. We all believe that in Friend's and each of our individual's pet's life reality and in whatever form they choose, animals DO reincarnate!
Use any information that resonates with you.

Physical Death:

Each physical body provides an opportunity to depart, whether it ages, is physically broken or ill, or just wears out. It's part of the trading spaces process. Upgrading to a healthier body is a necessity for our beloved animals, birds, fish or reptiles that have shorter life spans, so they can continue sharing your life's journey.

If you are reading this book prior to the impending passage of the love of your life, KNOW that death and transition is the **first** step in reuniting with you. This fact will help you during the transition and waiting process.

During the transition process, your pet's physical body will be in conflict with its soul's love for you and wanting to stay with you. Sometimes when a pet is preparing to pass, and you are asking them to hang on for your sake, the pet will walk away from you, not look at you in your eyes, or even stay in another room. Sometimes you will see that pet sitting at a window or door staring out as if they are memorizing their last earthly view. Since your beloved companion is so connected to you, even crying depletes your pet's energy and hampers their ability to transition in the best way possible!

Give your "baby" permission to do as they so choose, honor their journey so they can be a part of yours quicker! It's all about mutual love and respect, although this is so hard to do in critical times.

Affirmation to assist your pet's transition:
The affirmation below will assist your cherished companion in transitioning easier and without horrific physical complications. Hold its front paws with your hands or place your hand on the pet's body near its heart, look into its eyes if possible and ask with your heart or out loud:

"Fill in blank with Pet's name, I love you. I honor, respect and support your choices. From the love in my heart, I send you my life force energy to use as you so choose."

(This can be voiced out loud or silently, and said one time or as often as you wish.)

Your intent with this declaration will assist in making your pet's transition as gentle as possible. It is imperative that you use the words "you so choose' so your pet can use the additional energy boost to either cross over or to get better--- Then it's THEIR choice!

Usually after you have said this phrase, at some point in time before they cross the Rainbow Bridge, your pet will create a tender memory moment as their way of acknowledging your love and releasing them to complete this time's soul's path.

A client's cat was extremely ill for months and stayed alone in her bed in a dark corner. Days after the client started saying the affirmation above, her cat got up, came over to sit in her lap and purred for the first time since her illness began. She calmly went to sleep (unassisted) in the safe haven of her owner's love.

Also, before or during the timeframe when your pet starts withdrawing its life force energy, which is usually 24 – 48 hours prior to leaving its body, you can see its aura gradually diminish and you can ask your pet if it is going to reincarnate.

Prayer for Reincarnation:

Hold your pet's front paws with your hands or place your hand on the pet's body near its heart, look into its eyes if possible and ask with your heart or out loud:
"I ask and it is my intent to know if we will be together again in this lifetime. Will you return to live with me again in this lifetime?"

Your heart will hear the answer. If you do not receive an answer, it may be due to the fact that your pet has not made their decision yet. If you do not receive an answer that you feel is clear and factual due to the emotional upheaval that everyone is experiencing, then use the prayers set forth in a later section, to receive a response after your pet is on the other side

Although physical death may and does seem so very heart wrenching and permanent, you must remember that it is the FIRST step toward reincarnation.

• **Prayer for Confirmation Signs**

I ask and it is my intent to know if _____is going to return to be with me in this lifetime. Please give me 3 signs within the next three days that I can easily understand that allows me to know in my heart whether or not my beloved pet is coming back to me in this lifetime. Thank you.

• **Prayer to Assist Your Pet in Reincarnating if He Chooses**

I ask and it is my intent to send _____(the deceased pet's name)_from the love in my heart, my life force energy to use as he/ she so chooses. So be it, it is done.

If your pet is going to choose to reincarnate, providing extra energy from the love in your heart will help them transition from the other side back to earth more easily. The key is to state "to use as they so choose." Then your pet will determine the perfect timing for their healthy return.

I know a lady that wanted her "four legged baby" back so badly that when it reincarnated it was in less than perfect physical health and form.

73

Although her "fur child" hurried to return to her, the results from rushing the timing were less than desirable. SO be sure to state "to use as you so choose" and be patient in order for your pet to make the most appropriate and healthiest reentry.

I even wrote a pet loss gift book about my dog Friend, *"the Dog with a "B" on His Bottom,"* to prove that your prayers will be answered in perfect timing! So "B"elieve and "B" inspired to hold onto your hope!

How many times can an animal reincarnate?

- Each pet has its individual soul's path as you do. Sometimes a pet will only be with you one time in your entire life. That single incarnation is their "path" with you. You will know within your heart if your pet is returning to you. You will also know if he isn't reincarnating. Your strong human animal soul bond and intuition creates this "knowing."

- An animal can choose multiple reincarnations within their human companion's lifespan. The more learning and teaching you have to experience together (key word), the more often your pet will reincarnate or "walk in" to evolve with you.

- A pet who is an old soul, has been here many times and completed his path with you does not have to return. It's that pet's choice to reincarnate again if he wants to continue to accompany you on your life's journey.

- Sometimes a young animal that has unexplained medical problems or lots of medical conditions will choose to depart earth early in life. Their souls are getting rid of the "sick" body in order to exchange it for a healthier one. Upon the reincarnate's reentry, their new more durable fur, finned or feathered form can live longer to share a more extended lifetime with you.

- We have seen on numerous occasions, animals that reincarnate only to stay until their owner passed over. One touching story was about a stray kitten that just "showed up!" It came to sit in her owner's lap while she was wheelchair bound during the end stage diseases of her life. When the owner passed, within 3 days, that perfectly healthy cat died in her sleep to join her owner.
- Sometimes an animal will reincarnate to mirror the medical condition or take on the same health issues of its owner. Their medical plight will often help their owner learn more about treating their own disorder.

Can a pet return as a human?
- According to my experience and those of numerous renowned animal and interspecies communicators, pet psychics and intuitives, animals do not reincarnate in human form because an animal's body has a lower energy frequency than a human body. Energy can reform at a like or lower level, but is not usually able to reincarnate into an energy frequency higher than the original spirit.

On the other hand in the Yogic view, there are 8.4 million life times that souls evolve through, beginning with the lowest life forms. In this Yogic belief system, it is understood that an animal can and will eventually become a human. According to this Yogic theory, sometimes an animal soul that becomes a human prematurely, before it has learned enough lessons to truly evolve, can reincarnate as a person that exhibits excessive "beast like" qualities.

In regards to the information above and in this entire book, always go with your inner guidance, experiences and what resonates with you.
- I am aware of animals that have behaved like humans. Human energy can adjust down into a lower frequency, so it is possible for a human to retain a pet body for a return incarnation. However, most likely a human may "over soul" a pet. Usually older individuals that have transitioned will "over soul" a pet.

As an example, a friend had a dog that emulated all of the old characteristics of her husband who had previously passed away. Therefore the husband's spirit was contributing his guidance and past knowledge to the current pet as an "over soul", (i.e. a soul in heaven who provides guidance and supervises over the earthly being).

A pet being "over souled" will display more "acts like someone" traits rather than initiating within your heart that **deep** certain knowing that "it's my old pet reincarnated."

Can my animal reincarnate into another pet form?

- Soul connected spirit guide and or guardian pets will select the most appropriate animal form to accompany you during the particular life phase that you will be sharing.
- Your pet may reincarnate either as a male or female or as a different breed of the same or another species. That lop-eared bunny love bug you had as a child may choose to return as your female "tigger kitty" then as a male Great Dane, and later as your horse when you're an adult. Be open minded. Do not always expect the exact same physical image or gender.
- More prevalent however is the fact that your pet will usually reincarnate within the same species and within your animal preferences. After all, they know you well! They will always have or exhibit a special identifiable characteristic to insure you recognize them!

I prefer prick eared rough coated female red border collies. My "new" Friend is a male (with lots of female tendencies) prick eared medium coated tri color. Close enough! ☺- especially with that bright white "B" on his bottom like my signature!

Can my new puppy or a mature dog that was born BEFORE my dog died, be my pet reincarnated?

YES! At times your pet's new body will arrive on earth before your pet's old body passes away. This is a pre arranged agreement (made in Heaven) between your original, to be deceased pet's spirit and the "delivery soul."

After your original pet's spirit departs his old body, he then "walks into" (i.e. transfer his soul's energy) into the "new model" that was created and delivered in advance to await his return.

The "delivery pet soul" (like an auto company's driver delivering a new car) then returns to Heaven (the manufacturer), having completed his "delivery" job of transporting your pet's new body onto earth. Sometimes this is an immediate process; at times it takes several weeks. Human "walk-ins" have many websites that can be found on the Internet that can further define and explain this process.

Therefore the mature dog that was waiting at the pound may have been your pet's new body delivered years in advance before your deceased pet was ready to go. The new body just arrived earlier than expected!

However the transfer of the contracting pet soul's energy walking in after its body's death is the same, and the "delivery soul" just had to wait around a little longer for the exchange to occur. (see the story following about Darby and Riinna)

A "soul braid" occurs when a deceased pet's spirit blends with a current living pet's body and energy. The current pet then acts like and has characteristics of both animals.

A "walk-in" and "soul braid" transition timeframe can occur immediately, overnight or over a few months time. Your heart will understand, feel and inherently know what is transpiring.

How long does reincarnation take?

• Your pet's return can be as short as several hours or longer. Be patient with whatever timeframe they require to acquire that new body, OR have prearranged to be able to return to you. Sometimes your childhood pet doesn't return until you are an adult.

• To reiterate: It's possible that your old dog "walks in" to that new puppy or 3 month old stray or 9 year old rescue dog that has been "waiting" at the shelter in literally a heartbeat! If your pet is a "walk-in", the "delivery" (body) can come in MANY forms and ages, because the "delivery" body was custom made for your pets "walk-in" return. Age is not a factor.

Communicating with your pet on the other side:
- Ways to communicate with your pet on the other side include:
    Meditate and ask within your heart
    Use an animal or interspecies communicator, pet psychic,
        medium, intuitive or clairvoyant.
    Listen to your inner guidance and knowing
You can use these methods or others that resonate with you in any combination.

- The state of energy in which an animal passes affects the timeframe in which an animal communicator can contact your pet's energy. Some very ill animals need to restore their original energy base before they are able to transmit information across the veils because they have a weak "signal." Other animals transmit from the other side loud and clear the minute they vacate the old body.

- If you are not comfortable with your inner guidance and or want further information to formulate your opinion, an animal or interspecies communicator, pet psychic, clairvoyant or spiritual medium often times can alert you to the fact that your pet will be or is returning and in what general form. Some can also provide other information that might include the fact that your pet may already be here and waiting for you to find them! Every gifted communicator will advise you to only use the information that resonates with your soul!

- On occasion your pet will leave little signs for you from the other side. You'll find toys in the floor that you thought you had previously stored. You'll hear noises of your other animals playing with the passed pet's spirit as an "imaginary friend."

- You can sense, smell, hear or feel your pet from the other side. You are <u>not</u> "crazy."
These will be distinct, yet random incidents and feelings that your heart and soul **will** recognize!

- Your pet will visit in your dreams.

- When you are crying nonstop, praying or just wondering if your beloved four legged family member is okay, sometimes your pet will cause a commotion or distraction that you **know in your heart** is their response to let you know that they are just fine. A friend's deceased dog would use his energy to knock his pictures off her table when she was upset, to let her know that he was still watching over her from the other side.

The stages of your animal's return
Grieving:

- Initially you really miss your pet more than a mere animal loss. You recognize he had a "special bond" with you and that you were blessed to share life with him. You feel "we aren't done yet." Feeling that "special bond," "blessed" and "aren't through" is your soul's recognition and understanding that your pet has a shared soul growth involvement with you in this lifetime. You have things to learn "together."

- At times you may be angry due to the manner in which your pet died. The sooner you release your anger, the more receptive you are to receiving your new buddy. <u>Your anger blocks and stalls your pet's energy movement back into your life</u>. As soon as you can, celebrate the fact that your beloved companion is on the way back home. Your beloved pet has to get a replacement body to keep on "keeping on" with you!

- During bereavement, if you still feel that you want to hold onto your pet's beds, bowl and toys, collar, et al, usually there is a deeper reason.
Your inner guidance inherently knows that they will be back. Just keep his possessions in a safe place to let him know you understand he'll return and is not forgotten.

- Your pet's return is drawing closer when you are:
  "Seeing" their energy out of the corner of your eye
  >Seeing them in recurrent dreams
  "Feeling" their presence like laying in your lap, jumping on the bed or leaving toys out
  "Hearing" them doing something familiar (licking fur, playing with one of your current live pets)
  Experiencing other little "announcements" that YOU understand!

You are not going nuts!

Your pet is providing more obvious frequent notice that their spirit's energy is adapting back into the earth's energy and they are on the way and everything is and will be fine!

Reconnection: How will we get back together?
- Listen to and trust when and where your intuition and inner guidance leads you to initiate your reconnection.

Act immediately! Do not delay the timing and guidance of your inner urgings when your heart compels or incessantly nags you to search for your pet's new body form.

- You will instinctively be led to, and will "know" whether to look for a puppy, a rescue animal, in an animal shelter, on an internet search or in a newspaper ad. Your pet may just wander up and appear out of "nowhere." Someone may call you to "come see" this wonderful fur, finned or feathered creature that was "just turned in." GO! Have you left yet?

- If you are new to listening to your inner guidance, let's say this again: Never overlook the little details and just pass them off as not worthy of attention. Follow through on all information presented to you, **at the time it is presented** and trust it is correct. All the myriad domino effects lead to your pet! **There are no coincidences!**

- Do NOT be discouraged by "he's already taken or been adopted," or sold or not available. If you KNOW in your heart that this is YOUR pet, be steadfast, keep going forward and do not be discouraged or deterred by what you perceive as current roadblocks.

When it's your animal companion, all things will just "work out" in some of the most interesting, amazing and _unbelievable_ ways for you to be together again!
An "adopted" pet may never get picked up, a deposit never honored, people change their minds! Read some of the following stories!

- If you don't have that "certain knowing" in your heart and the details don't work out for you to get a particular animal, that's the Universe letting you know, it's not the right one! It's NOT your reincarnated pet!
The Universe actually helps steer you by making SURE that you don't get the wrong pet! When it's the correct reincarnate, the Universe will arrange to make all things possible to bring your companion home!

Recognition: How will I recognize MY pet?
- Do NOT allow anyone who is outside your heartfelt circle tell you it's your pet reincarnated!!! ONLY you and those very close to your pet's soul when he/she was alive will actually feel and know that true soul recognition! I could FEEL Friend in my heart! But I actually missed the "B" on his hip because I was so caught up in and overwhelmed by my emotions!

My close friends, who were an integral part of my previous reincarnates lives, immediately recognized when they saw the video, that it was MY Friend returning home to me!
They pointed out that the "B" in Friend's fur looked like my signature, and that God obviously knew I needed "confirmation."

81

- A visual recognition story: One Saturday afternoon, a lady felt strong inner urges to drive to a shelter to find a dog to fill her heart's void until (she thought) her beloved pet reincarnated. When she and her husband pulled into the parking lot, her soul recognition kicked in.

There, walking across the parking lot toward the shelter was her reincarnated pet on a leash with someone else! Coincidentally, the Universe had prearranged for another family to take her reincarnated puppy to the shelter at that very moment. They were turning the puppy in for adoption.
Timing is everything! She immediately adopted HER dog!

- Your pet will also choose you in order to assist you in recognizing their reincarnated form! They will choose you under any and all circumstances. They know you, and there is no doubt about it when they pick you! This fact applies even if they are living with another individual before coming back into your life.

Judy visited her cousin and was adopted immediately by her cousin's "Westie." After Judy left that dog mourned, whined, would not eat, etc, so much that Judy's cousin finally gave her the Westie for the "dog's sake."

Loui was happily reunited with "her person" Judy for 17 more years.

Confirmation:
- Look into your pet's eyes, the windows of their soul.
Your heart will **know** them and **feel** the connection you share and have shared. It's **soul recognition**!

- Ask your pet questions with your soul and listen to their answers with your heart.

- Your pet will bond with you right away, almost immediately! Even if they are a "walk-in "or "soul braid" as illustrated in one of the following stories, you will still KNOW it's your pet as they make their spirit's transition into their new body!

- Reincarnates respond immediately to all the old "things." Often times your new pet even responds to your old pet's name and knows exactly where all the old pet's possessions are located.

Sometimes they recognize their old home! In one of the following stories, a young pup recognized his old home and tried to get out of the car while riding past it on the way to the owner's new house. (see Union Jack's story in the next section)

- Their emotional behavior traits and physical mannerisms are uncannily similar, right down to sleeping in the same location in "that funny position," turning their head a certain way, liking the exact food (like eating ice cubes), and even disliking or liking the same pet in your current household, etc.

- Your "new" reincarnated animal (puppy, kitten, bunny, ferret, bird, foal, or Beta Fish, etc) will act like an adult much sooner than expected and will display fewer "new baby" behaviors and attitudes.

- A "walk in" or "over-soul" pet's traits will be uncannily the same or VERY similar from the get go. You'll have very few doubts that's it's your returned forever buddy!

- Current household animals that lived with the transitioned pet will recognize the "new" old soul. The reincarnates also will have some of the same grudges and disputes with the same animals. Friend always got along with Mikey; however he never liked "Ugly, the most beautiful cat of them all." They still don't get along. I had hoped Heaven would have expanded his patience!

- Oftentimes when your pet comes back, they will embody a new trait that you had been hoping they would have. These new traits may also contribute to your future path together.

As an example, my previous "Sunday dogs" were never "child friendly" because they lived with a single adult and were never exposed to children.

New Friend is a child/ people magnet. He thinks he's "human." The Universe obviously knew that this will be a wonderful trait for his paw/book signings, guest appearances for fundraising and pet therapy work with children and visitations in health care facilities!

Reuniting: "I'm Home!"
No matter where your pet's energy is, whether they reincarnate or not, your beloved finned, furry or feathered soul connected companion will always be a part of your heart forever and always!!!
Because
Love is never ending!

Choose hope!
Your companion might be just a heartbeat away!
and soon you'll feel
"I'm Home!"
Just ask *Friend!* The Dog with **my** "B" on His Bottom!

MORE
Wonderful Reincarnation Stories
from Around the World!

©Diane Lewis Photography

Revel Comes Back as Sidewinder
Kim Young

In 2006 my young Australian shepherd, Revel,
died in a tragic accident on our farm.
I experienced some of the darkest days I've ever known!
I remember carrying his lifeless body back to my house and
crying until I physically couldn't cry anymore. I remember
praying and praying to God and begging for a miracle.
I pleaded with God to put life back into Revel and offered
anything I could think of in return. I felt like if there was a God
and He loved me and He loved Revel, God could have given
Revel's life back again. I became convinced that all my pleas
had fallen on deaf ears.

87

After he died, the first time I "saw" Revel was that same day. It was a fleeting glimpse that made me think I might be crazy. I had taken his body to the crematorium and staggered out of the building almost blinded by my tears. As I approached my truck, I saw him sitting in the front seat, beside my other dogs, just like he had so many times before. His image was there for and instant and then it was gone. I thought my eyes were playing tricks on me.

What I didn't understand at that time, was that seeing Revel's image was his way of telling me he was all right.

Leaving the crematorium was one of the hardest things I've ever had to do. Somehow in my mind I wanted to believe it was all a bad dream. If I never went home and never saw that he wasn't there, then I'd wake up and things would be okay.

My husband drove us around for hours because I simply couldn't bear the prospect of going home, opening the door to our home and not seeing him there to greet me as he had so many times before.

One of the greatest lows of my life was opening that door to nothing but darkness and silence. Feeling so hollow and empty, just as I stepped inside, I felt a strange warmth and love wash all over me. I turned to my husband and said, "He's here. I feel him." At that moment, I knew what I felt was pure love and that Revel was around me.

If I had any skepticism in my mind about yesterday's occurrence, the thing that happened next took it all away. From our bedroom, my female Aussie, Chelsea, started barking. It was her play bark, not an alarm bark. I walked in the room to check on her and there she was playing with a toy that was Revel's which I had hidden in my spare bedroom since I couldn't bear to look at them.

Revel normally spread toys all over our house! That toy had been stored out of sight BEFORE I left. Chelsea and my other dogs had been with me. No one had been home, and the door to the spare bedroom was tightly shut. There was NO way it could now be in my bedroom with Chelsea playing with it clearly with another dog.

I didn't see her imaginary friend with my eyes, but clearly Chelsea saw Revel as she bowed and bounced around his toy. When he was alive, this is how they played together. They were best friends. I just knew in my heart that Revel was doing everything within his power to show me he hadn't left me.

I felt a blur of emotions. I was so grateful for his "visit" but I was still devastated. I relived the morning of his death so many times in my mind playing the "what if" game. What if I hadn't gone to the barn that morning? What if any of a million other things had happened that wouldn't have put him in that place in that particular time when he died? I would play it out differently in my mind a thousand times and try to change the outcome. I would relive his last day and beat myself up over and over again for not playing Frisbee with him that afternoon. It was his favorite game. I had put it off that day thinking we had all the time in the world.

The day before Revel died, my car was stolen. That seemed like a pretty big deal at the time. I'd spent the day dealing with the insurance company and police and hadn't taken time to lay with him. He'd waited patiently all day lying curled up next to my feet at my desk.

When Revel died, I realized how unimportant some "things" are. I'd spent my last day with him worrying about a stupid car because I thought he and I had years together. Ironically, I got the car back within about 24 hours of his death. I could have cared less. I would have given that car up a million times to have Revel back.

In the following weeks, during my darkest hours, when grief would overwhelm and paralyze me, strange things would happen in my house. Revel would take his toys out of the spare bedroom numerous times. I would put them up and would come back inside only to find them out again. The TV would turn itself on during the middle of the night. Pictures of my dogs would fall off of the wall and off of my desk but would never break despite landing on a ceramic tile floor. Doors moved with no one near them to move them. It was never frightening because when those things happened, I felt a wave of love wash over me.

I would "see" him only one more time. One night I was walking in the pasture at dusk and out of the corner of my eye I saw a bouncing red bob tailed dog galloping out of sight. It was my Revel.

Chelsea saw him a lot. There were multiple instances in which she played with a dog that we couldn't physically see yet she saw clearly. One night as I lay in bed, I woke up and felt physical pressure on my feet. Revel always slept on my feet. For that moment I knew he was there.

I started to think I was crazy and had lost it.

People don't talk about this stuff and most people I tried to broach it with were not receptive and put it off to my extreme grief. Fortunately, my husband, previously a skeptic, saw it too, so I knew it was real. I'm sure my dearest Revel, knowing how skeptical I was, knew he had to go to extra measures to get my attention and to make me believe.

The sadder I was, the more he did to show me he was here and that he hadn't left me. In hindsight, I also realize he was trying to communicate his plan to me. As more things happened in my house, I became convinced he was trying to tell me something. I so desperately wanted to talk to him and know what he was trying to communicate.

As an extreme skeptic I had scoffed at the idea of animal communicators and pet psychics. To actively seek out an animal communicator was a MAJOR deal for me. Actually communicating with and getting information from a dead pet was something I had never believed in.

I decided to use a well respected West Coast communicator since I lived on the East Coast. This appealed to me because in my mind it was a true test. There was NO way on earth that this person could know anything about me or my dog ahead of time.

I was <u>very</u> guarded in speaking to her and only gave minimal information. She actually only requested descriptive information - basically what my dog physically looked like and his name so she would recognize him when she called him. That was it!

With his name and description she started communication with Revel and I was blown away! She was definitely speaking to my dog and she described the subtle nuances of his behavior that only I would have known. She knew things we had done together that only Revel and I would have known. She described him perfectly even calling him "impetuous" and saying that he couldn't sit still while she was talking to him. That was so Revel! She also knew about what he'd been doing in the house moving things, and she was over 3,000 miles away!

My mind was set at ease. First, it was very clear to me that Revel was fine. Second, she told me he said he was coming back to me because we had a lot of things planned to do together that we hadn't done yet. I was so happy (and yet so confused) that I couldn't believe it.

I asked how I would know him. She said that Revel indicated that I would KNOW when it was him.
She also told me that he wouldn't wait long to come back.

I didn't know what to think. This was the best news I'd ever gotten and yet the skeptical side of me didn't want to believe this was possible.

On the other hand, how did someone across the country know the things this woman had known about my dog.

I decided then and there, if there was the slightest possibility that Revel could come back, I would give up my skeptical ways and try to be more open minded.

I was not going to shortchange Revel. He loved me in his life on earth and he was loving me from the other side after he died

He was trying so hard to communicate with me that it was time for me to trust what I felt,
what I'd seen, what I'd heard
and what I KNEW in my heart!

Revel was coming back to me!
As an aside for those that don't believe in animal communication and pet psychics, I was so stunned by the accuracy in the communication with and from Revel, I later returned to this communicator multiple times to talk to my living dogs. Each time, I was amazed at the accuracy of information provided.

After that communication, I felt magnetized to my computer. I needed to start looking, now! Especially since Revel said I would KNOW when it was him. For the first time since his death, I became convinced by the knowing in my heart that he would be coming back to me as an Aussie. I just felt it!

I looked at other breeds, but they didn't feel right. Every time I took a step in the right direction, my compulsion grew stronger. When I was sure he was coming back as an Aussie, I started looking at Aussie rescue websites. I saw beautiful dogs, but none of them "spoke to me." Their stories were heartwarming, but they weren't Revel. I can't explain it better than that. I just knew.

As I looked at adult dogs, I inherently felt he was coming back to me as a puppy. He was young when he died. He told the communicator we had a lot to do together so I was sure he would be young again. Friends would send me more pictures of litters of puppies than I could look at and I'd submerge myself looking at websites. I would see beautiful litters of pups and wonderful dogs, but I just knew none were him.

"Knowing in my soul" Revel was coming back as an Aussie puppy; I became even more obsessed with looking at rescue and kennel's websites. Sometimes I'd sit up all hours of the night or wake up at night and be drawn to get out of bed and go to the Internet to look at puppies.

I then began a very systematic search. There was a web listing of Aussie kennels alphabetized by states and countries. I started there, working my way through them one by one. At first, I thought maybe he'd come back to me through his first life bloodlines. I looked at those kennels and things just "didn't feel right."

Every time I'd look through a website and get the feeling I wasn't on the right track, it was disheartening. The farther I made it down that list without feeling like I was right was very discouraging. I was exhausting my supply of places to search. I started to worry, what if I was wrong? What if the communicator was wrong? What if he couldn't come back?

Despite doubts, there was something inside of me that was stronger and compelled me to keep looking. I had to! And I did. I was through over 75% of the list, when I came to this kennel in Texas. I knew the kennel name due to the outstanding reputation of their working dogs.

I looked at their website and came to their stud dog's page which immediately magnetized me. The description of him was my ideal dog, it described my Revel. I knew this dog wasn't Revel, but I knew immediately that Revel would come back to me through him. <u>I just knew</u>.

After that, I didn't look at another website. I knew where he was coming from, I just didn't know when or how.

I contacted the owner to see if she had any current puppies sired by this dog. She didn't but she was expecting 3 litters within a few weeks, one of which would have this dog as its sire. That was the good news. The bad news was that this litter had an over a year old waitlist for his puppies.
There were already deposits on the upcoming pups and the owner said there was almost no hope that there would be enough pups for everyone already on the wait list,
much less a latecomer like me.

I decided to choose with all my heart to believe in the "miracle" of his return. I just clung to that!
and asked if I could send in a deposit anyway.

The pups were born in a few weeks. There were only 5 in the litter I was interested in. When they were a few days old, I saw their first photos. I recognized Revel immediately!

Their eyes were closed and they were in a pile, but out of this pile, this little red merle male seemed to be crawling out of the computer screen to get to me. I knew it was him.

Before I go further, I want to mention a couple of things. After talking to the communicator and starting on the path to find Revel, things stopped being moved in my house. I was still lonely and sad, but the overwhelming grief passed and I started to move forwards while I searched for him. I think he needed me to do that to be able to move forward himself.

Also after he died and I became convinced that he was still around, at times I would talk to him. I would tell him that I knew he was here, that I so missed touching and hugging him "in fur form." Revel took care of that too.

I had done fostering for Aussie rescue. After Revel died, I was asked to foster a delightful female Aussie. For a brief time I thought maybe she was him coming back to me, but my heart's "knowing" quickly realized that wasn't the case. I adored her, but she wasn't my dog.

Revel had sent her to me to fill the void while he was gone. Ironically, she arrived a few days after his death and was adopted a few days before his return. I am sure that was Divine and Revel's intervention.

Although I knew which puppy was Revel, I was still last on the deposit list. How could this possibly work out? There were more great signs. When all 3 litters were born, the breeder told me something occurred that she hadn't seen in all of her years raising puppies; almost all the pups were male. Apparently a lot of folks with deposits wanted females so they were removed from the list.

In many Aussie litters, the merles are first to go. Yet as people with deposits made their selections, that red merle pup wasn't chosen. Surprisingly, one day I received an email saying the red pup was mine if I still wanted him. I asked when I could come get my dog!

At 7 weeks old, we drove days to Texas to get him. I couldn't fathom waiting another week for him to be old enough to fly or much less trusting him to the airlines. I'd lost him once. I wasn't going to lose him again.

People ask if I was worried I'd get there and be disappointed with the pup. I definitely worried about what if I'd been wrong. What if I got there and this pup didn't like me? What if we didn't bond? I had chosen him based purely on this overwhelming feeling that that was my Revel. I had to trust that. So many things had come into play to make that pup mine, that in my heart, I didn't think I could be wrong.

We drove through the night to get to Texas. We had arranged a hotel for the first night there and were due to pick up the pup the first thing the next morning. We ended up arriving early and it was all I could do not to stop by and pick up my puppy a day early. I hardly slept that night.

Early the next day, we drove to the breeder's house. Introductions were made and then she said something like "let me show you your puppy."

She went inside and got him and set him down on the ground. He immediately walked over to me and sat down in front of me and looked up as if to say, "Where have you been? Let's get on with it...." In that instant, when our eyes met, all doubt was gone. I was looking into my Revel's eyes again.

When the communicator spoke to Revel, I asked if he wanted to be called Revel again. He said together we'd pick a new name. For weeks, I'd written out dozens of possible names and even had my list of names with me.

When I saw my puppy, I knew his name was Sidewinder. That wasn't even a name on my list, but I knew it was the right name. For this reincarnation, my Revel is Sidewinder.

Physically, they don't look the same. They do have eerily similar mannerisms and the same eyes. A dear friend once told me that the "eyes are the window to the soul." That makes sense to me because clearly it's his same soul.
His packaging is just a little different this time around.

When Sidewinder came home, the emptiness left the house. I'm no longer sad when I see Revel's pictures. I'm just looking at pictures of his old body. He's here now, in a new one!

One thing that has blown me away is what Sidewinder knew from the get go, as if he was starting off where Revel left off. He entered my house at 7 weeks old with a Frisbee obsession, despite never having seen a Frisbee before. He found his old toys in the spare bedroom and immediately had them back out all over the house.

He lies on the back of the sofa draped like a cat, like Revel did. He sleeps on my feet at night and is always near me, like Revel. He even destroys his stuffed toys in order to pull the squeaker out in the same methodical way as Revel did.

Sometimes both my husband and I call him Revel by mistake and Sidey responds just the same.

Other interesting things: Revel was being trained for agility. He hadn't been trialed yet, however impressively he never made the same mistake twice. From the get go, Sidewinder has displayed that same catlike prowess and brightness. At an agility seminar the instructor commented: "he never makes the same mistake twice." Clearly Sidey was relying on what he'd learned as Revel.

They say little children see auras and energy naturally. My 3 year old niece was looking at my dogs' pictures and told me she liked Sidewinder's picture. At first I was confused because there aren't any pictures of Sidewinder. What she was looking at were old pictures of Revel. She told me with certainty that she was looking at Sidewinder. Since the dogs do not look physically similar, I believe she was seeing the same energy.

That's just one more incident to reinforce what I absolutely believe to be true. My Sidewinder is a reincarnated version of my Revel. Almost every day something shows me my 2 dogs are the same soul. God heard my prayers as I cried over Revel's lifeless body. He brought him back to me. Since then, many things have changed in my life and my mind has been opened to and aware of things I never believed possible.

My world is a much more beautiful place because I know death isn't final, and that the Universe holds endless possibilities when we open our heart and minds to just trust and believe...

©Diane Lewis Photography

Darby "Walks In" to Riina
ANN

Or August 27th 2005 at approximately 11:30 pm I held my special sweet heart dog Darby in my arms as the Vet helped her pass on. She was nine years old and I wanted oh so many more years with her. I wrote a poem after I got home from the vets office. I was completely devastated and could not imagine my life without Darby.

DARBY
Kurpas' Darby N Red Velvet
July 24, 1996 - August 27, 2005

My Angel Darby

I smell a fragrance from the valley carried in a breeze

The wind softly touches my fur then moves through the trees

My eyes see golden leaves and clouds of winter white

Tiny angels with halos will visit me each night

I stand on a soft cloud a rainbow overhead

An angel with glorious wings is stroking my head

As a delicate wind enshrouds me a soft stroke on my cheek

I've been touched by an angel and now I am at peace

Love has no boundaries

I'll watch over you

I'll wait for you

I held my sweet Darby in my arms telling her how much
I loved her and it was OK for her to go, as the vet
helped her pass to a beautiful place.
A part of me went with her. I miss her so.

In October on a Sunday night, about 2 months after Darby passed; I was searching the internet on pet loss sites to help find some solace. I came across a web site that had a page on pet reincarnation. I think I read that page at least a dozen times. I had never really thought about the possibility of pets reincarnating but I needed to know more.

First thing Monday morning I called the animal communicator that had this article on her site to set up an appointment with her for a consultation. I had to wait until the following Friday. That was a long week for me. Friday at the appointment time I called her. When she answered the phone she was laughing and said that Darby is a chatter box and knew the appointment time and had been bugging her.

She began to tell me things she could not possibly have known about Darby since I had not given her any information prior to the appointment. She was right on with so many things she told me. I was so emotional during this call. Close to the end of the session I asked her if Darby planned to return to me.

She said absolutely and that Darby had been with me through many lifetimes. I was so excited and skeptical all at the same time. I had never dreamed this could happen. So I asked her how does this happen? She said she felt there are a few ways this can happen.

According to that communicator's knowledge: One, you find a litter of puppies you are interested in and in that litter you pick a puppy. Another way is to find an older dog, not old, but older then a puppy. Another way is that a puppy will be born and Darby will guide you to her.

I chose to look for a puppy that had made a "walk in" agreement with Darby. Then I was to contact the animal communicator and she would do a reading with Darby and the puppy.

I could not imagine in my mind how this could possibly work. Darby had some requirements she told the animal communicator. Darby wanted to have a tail, be female again if possible, she did not want to be white and she wanted to be healthy.

When she was a little over a year old Darby had vaccinosis caused by her Rabies vaccine. I'd worked with Darby keeping her as healthy as possible for 8 + years. Her body finally gave up. Being healthy was very important to her.

Personally, I had decided on getting a Finnish Lapphund.
I had done a lot of research on the breed and knew this was
the breed I wanted. Of course I picked a breed that is quite
rare here in the US. I started contacting people in Finland. Now
I do not speak Finnish so this was an adventure all by itself.

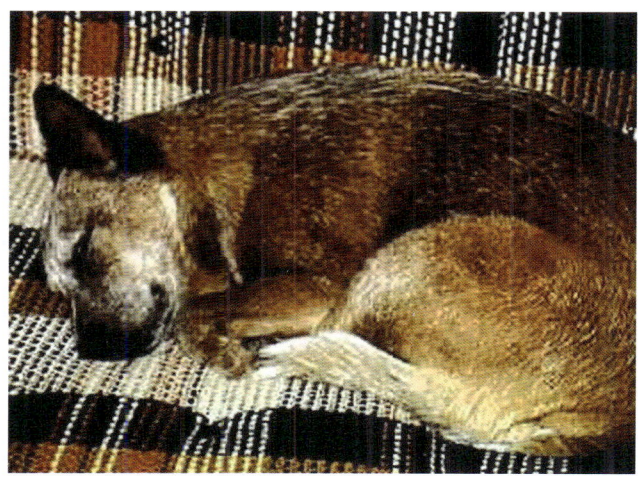

I had located a couple of litters through kennels I thought would be reputable. I had the animal communicator do a reading on a couple of puppies and the answer was they had not made a "walk in" arrangement with Darby.

January of 2006 a litter was born in Denmark that I was very interested in and I contacted the owner who (thank heaven) spoke English. There were 12 pups in the litter, 7 females and 5 males. The owner and I had lots of conversations. She knew what I wanted in structure and temperament and of course a female. Finnish Lapphund temperaments are wonderful. They are very sweet, kind and affectionate dogs just like my Darby is. Australian Cattle dogs can be a handful in many ways but my Darby was very sweet.

So as the puppies grew the owner sent me pictures every week and I looked at female puppy pictures. The puppy I picked was also the female that the puppy's guardian had picked for me or thought I would like. It was a difficult decision since all the pups were very cute.

Reincarnation is not a subject that many can embrace and I had not yet gone through the process so how could I feel with total assurance it can actually happen.

One day I got brave and told the owner I was hoping this puppy would be my sweet Darby's reincarnated soul. She was so cool and totally believed in reincarnation.

I contacted the animal communicator to do the reading for me to see if this puppy's soul had contracted with Darby to be the new reincarnation body. The answer was yes and the animal communicator said Darby was so excited and loved the little girl we had picked.

I was so very excited and began making arrangements to get the pup to the US. Several things happened that delayed getting her to. She finally arrived in Denver.

Riina was not feeling too good when we got her. She had a bladder infection and an upper respiratory infection most likely due to the long flight and the climate change.

The first time I saw her I was very emotional and the thoughts of having my sweet Darby back was overwhelming. She was adorable. Knowing that Riina was not feeling very well, I asked the animal communicator to speak with Darby and tell her to wait until I got Riina over her health issues.

I was told there is no time in heaven as it is here so not to worry. It was me that could hardly wait for this transition to begin.

From the beginning Riina's temperament was very aloof with us. Very unlike puppy behavior, especially a Finnish Lapphund puppy.

I watched her like a hawk and anticipated everything she did looking for any passed traits I could recognize of Darby. I kept thinking this is not going to happen because I saw nothing that I could recognize as a Darby trait.

Riina was a puppy that didn't want to play ball, give hugs or kisses, or care if she was with you. She pretty much did her own thing. She was very aloof. I came to realize and understand later there was a reason she was this way.

If you think about it, why would Riina want to become attached to us when our agreement was to move on after Darby's spirit "walked into" her body.

One afternoon I was sitting on the couch and Riina had lain down in the hallway. I could see her from where I was sitting and I called her to me, clapping my hands and encouraging her to come to me. She just looked at me, typical Riina reaction. She didn't move and went off to sleep. In about 5 minutes she woke up and ran to me jumped on my lap, placed her legs around my neck and began kissing my face and pressed her little chest against me. Her tail was wagging like crazy. Talk about heart pouncing emotion and the tears were streaming down my face.

I KNEW IN MY HEART THIS WAS DARBY. This was the first sign the transition had begun. The next few months that followed I recognized more and more of Darby.

There were times when I knew it was Riina one minute and Darby the next. I asked the animal communicator why it was taking so long and she said that Darby's spirit was indeed popping in and out of the delivery body.

Since Riina and Darby have very strong personalities sometimes the "walk in" and "soul braiding" process will take more time (some soul transitions happen right away while others can take months), for each of the participating soul's to adjust to their initial agreement.

One afternoon I had Riina outside with me and I threw the ball for her to chase. Now Riina would just look at me as if to say if you want it you go get it. Well this afternoon Riina did the Darby roo roo, fetched the ball and brought it back to me and was ready to go again with another roo roo, which means throw the ball. That was a definite Darby trait she did all the time in her past life.

Other things that Darby used to do was after she had eaten,

she would pick up her bowl and bring it to me as if to say (got anymore)? One evening right after feeding, she brought her dish to me. I knew that was Darby. Another trait was when I was sitting she would rest her head on my knee and stare into my eyes with so much love. Rinna soon became so affectionate, happy, content and always at my side. I was thrilled!

I am blessed to have Darby show so many traits from her past life to me. In the beginning or when the transition began, it was so obvious to my husband and me when Darby was with us and when Riina was here. Definite things that Darby used to do she was doing them again all on her own.

Love Like time has no boundries when seen through the eyes of our dogs.

Darby   I'm home   Riina

2008© Wayne M. Clarke of Zinalmage.ws

I asked the animal communicator to do another reading because I wanted to know how she was doing and how she felt. These are her words from my sweet Darby.
"""Feels great inside and out... Very 'spiritual' if that makes sense to you... Loves her new body and said 'we did good'... Not you and I, you and HER... She is very happy. Like from the soul outward.... Like her being is happy""

Riina the delivery soul had moved on and Darby is with me again. She even comes to the name Darby even though I call her Riina Darby Do. I find it very hard to put into words the way I feel. This process is the most amazing thing that has ever happened in my life. It is a true blessing and a wonder to have my sweet Darby back with me again. My Riina Darby Do.

Luke Returns in Lloyd
Suzanne and Jessica Mills from Brisbane, Queensland, Australia

Luke our black and white border collie was adopted at 9 months old before Jessica was born. Luke was my biggest support throughout a 5 year family episode. He was my 'rock' and without him I would never had remained strong. Luke held our family together. He was a beautiful example of courage and strength who taught me to stand my ground.

My 11 years old "Luke" passed away in June 2007 after a battle with throat cancer. Luke was a well mannered dog and many people referred to him as a "gentleman of a dog." Before he died the homeopath who was treating Luke told me that Luke was worried about me as we had not finished our journey together. There were no borders available at the time and I was not ready for him to leave me.

A friend of a friend has a stunning black and white border named "Stormy." She also had recently rehabilitated an old rescue border named "Chloe." We believed that Chloe was pregnant to Stormy
(we were not really sure but she was eating heaps).
Five weeks later I was walking my spaniel past our veterinary clinic and the vet called me in to see a litter of lemon and white borders. They were beautiful and the owner asked me to consider adopting the last one. The puppy's owner's name was "Luke" which was quite a coincidence.

My daughter bonded with a lemon pup. He was beautiful but I did not buy him as my gut told me that Stormy was going to bring our Luke back into the world. How was I to decide? If I went with the yet to be born pups, how would I pick?

My daughter Jessica did not mind which pup we had so long as it was our Luke. I was very concerned that I would not see the signs. I chose not to get the lemon pup as there was a University exam that I needed to sit in within two days time and I was reluctant to leave a six week old pup alone for the whole day since he had just joined our household.

My friends were also trying to discourage me from taking the lemon pup as he was from a strong working line and I wanted a family pet. The exam was cancelled and when I called to reconsider the lemon puppy he was already adopted. Four weeks later, we found out that Chloe did not end up having puppies at all. The news that Chloe was not pregnant came on Jessica's 12th birthday. I asked Jessica how she felt about the lemon pup that we missed out on and she said that he was not interested in her and that it was her who went after him. Knowing that Chloe and Storm were not going to have pups in the foreseeable future we looked at a reputable and caring pups4sale site.

There were lots of black and white (our favorite) and other Border collie shades. Nothing caught our eye, although we drooled for a while and then decided to wait. The next day I found a litter of tri colors for sale about 200k from here. I emailed the kennel and told Jessica, but she was not at all interested. That night the owner sent a picture of the last little pup available.

Jessica was so besotted by him that she was unable to concentrate. We visited him on July 19. His human family was delightful and the pup came immediately to us. He was adorable! He was still with 3 litter mates and his mum & dad but when he met us he stayed close to us. Jess said it was as if he was saying: "Where have you been?
What took you so long?"
There were lots of coincidences surrounding this puppy. The son of the human family who bred the pup was also named "Luke" the same as my old BC. Plus, this pup was born on the 20th anniversary of my best friend's death May 26. The family made us a cup of tea and our little pup lay on the couch between us touching both of our thighs while ignoring his other littermates.

We brought him home that evening and he took himself to the doggy bed in my bedroom and has done so ever since, EXACTLY at 7 pm just as our old Luke would do when he was here. He has never cried or whined like new puppies do. He loves our home and the other pets we have.

115

Jess and I both had a few tears of joy that this pup is here. Jess tells me that for her it is far greater than normal love and their bond is extraordinary. We tried several different names for this new little man over the first week.

For one reason or another they didn't work and just didn't fit or match his personality.

After trying so many different names, we noticed that he always responded better to "L" names. We named him "Lloyd." His soul is familiar to us and he has adopted all of the good spots that Luke loved. At only 9 weeks of age this little bloke is very mature. He sure is an exceptional little pup and I really don't have to wonder much if the Universe has reunited us.

Luke was a master of 'fetch' and Lloyd at 9 weeks is already showing some talent. There were times when Luke was concentrating he would hold his tail in the most awkward unflattering position and we would laugh at him and call him "Dorkus." Well Lloyd has the same habit! I really am looking forward to the next year to really see what more Lloyd has to show us.

He has even started to sleep on the same pink and beige
quilt that Luke did. We're planning on taking him to the beach
as soon as he has finished his vaccinations,
I can't wait to see if he enjoys it as much as Luke did.
Somehow, I know he will!
I now understand that there was no need to panic over
these issues. It simply takes the time and trust in the Universe
when your dog's spirit is ready to return for you.
The time will be right and it will fit.
Love will find its way back.
It makes me feel so safe about my dad who passed and shared
almost the same birthday as Lloyd (2 days earlier) and my
mum who died on the day that Luke had his diagnosis.
There is much connection.

"Dorkus" tail

Well at 54 years of age I am finally learning to trust the Universe. I hope that grieving humans are able to find comfort in knowing that there is more to this Universe than what we are conditioned to see, and parts that we do not really understand. Your heart will always know and feel what is right.

Jody Girl Returns as Union Jack
Then Reincarnates a 3rd Time as Little Jack
Pete Newell, Sarasota FLA

In the early 1980s, I used to give the stock market report
on the radio. One day in October of 1982 when I turned on the
dirt road where the radio station was located, this beautiful
liver & white female English Springer spaniel puppy
came up to my car
and I immediately knew there was something special about her.
I mentioned this puppy encounter to my brother and he told
me he knew the girl who owned the puppy. She was a vet tech
who originally planned to breed this pup but had changed her
mind and was looking for a good home for her.

119

After my brother mentioned that I thought the female Springer pup was special, she decided to give her to me.   When I was bringing my new female Springer pup home "The Girl Is Mine" by Paul McCartney and Michael Jackson played on the car radio which brought a smile to my face.
I named her Jody Girl after a girl I knew in the bank.

In August of 1994, after giving me 12 wonderful years, my Jody Girl crossed over. I kept hearing "I Will Remember You" by Amy Grant on the radio. Here are some of the lyrics:
"Look in my eyes while you're near
Tell me what's happening here
See that I don't want to say good-bye
Our love is frozen in time
I'll be your champion and you'll be mine
I will remember, I will remember you."

It was my Jody's way of telling me that she didn't want to say good-bye and was coming back to me.
I missed my Jody Girl so much that I meditated and contacted the "other side." I was told "to wait" and the guides would let me know when the time was right for her return. They proceeded to show me a liver & white male Springer Spaniel which surprised me because he was so big and I was looking for a female. They even called him Jack which I thought was too extraordinary.
At the time, none of this made any sense to me.

During December of 1994, for three days, I was overwhelmed missing my Jody Girl and was constantly tearing up. On the third day I started to feel better and got back to normal. I wrote everything down in a diary. Looking back, ironically the day the intensity of my pain of losing Jody Girl eased up, was (unbeknownst to me at the time), the day my reincarnate Union Jack had been born - December 19, 1994!

In January of 1995, I had an overwhelming persistent inner urge to look in the classified ads and, sure enough, there was an ad for English springer spaniel pups.
I was thrilled because I didn't know anyone who actually bred quality Springer Spaniels locally.
It turned out that I knew Juli the breeder from the early 70s.

1630 OAK Street

SARASOTA HERALD-TRIBUNE / SATURDAY, JANUARY 28, 1995

6870 Dogs

DALMATIAN PUPS -AKC 10wks
old, champion bloodline, $300-
350 each. All shots. 792-7252

DOBERMAN PUP,
full blooded, $100.
Call 753-9487

ENGLISH Springer Spaniel Pups.
(3) males. Liver & white, AKC,
$375 each. Call 953-4304

When I showed up to look at the pups, I picked each one up.
One of the male pups wagged his tail when I held him,
so I knew it must be Jack. While sitting around with Juli and her
husband, they asked me what I was going to name him.
I told them Jack. The husband happened to mention the British
Flag was called the Union Jack and suddenly a light bulb went
on in my head. Finally! The name Jack made sense to me. The
Union Jack name brought it all together and it right because he
was an <u>English </u>Springer Spaniel!

When I got in my car to leave Juli's house after my initial meeting with Union Jack as a pup, the song "After All" came on the radio. It was the Universe's way, I feel, of letting me know Jody Girl had come back to me as Union Jack.

Here are some of the lyrics:
  "Well, here we are again;
    I guess it must be fate.
    We've tried it on our own,
    But deep inside we've known
    We'd be back to set things straight."
  "It all comes down to me and you.
    I guess it's meant to be,
    Forever you and me, after all."

Then the first day I brought Union Jack home, he ran up to my Jody Girl's bed and just stood in front of it and stared. A couple months later, I drove by my old house where I had lived with Jody Girl for most of her life and, all of a sudden, Jack got very excited and I thought he was going to jump through the car window. That's when I was convinced Jody Girl really had come back to me as Union Jack.
She recognized her old home!!

Six months before Union Jack's transition, his legs grew so weak I had to carry him up & down the stairs. I knew Jack was getting ready to cross over so I would hug and kiss him when I carried him.

In early February of 2008, my beloved Union Jack, after giving me 13 loving and faithful years, crossed over. I was devastated to put it mildly. I still am! Jack was my faithful and loving companion who blessed my life for 13 years.
I was listless and so lost without him.

The other side has always communicated with me by giving me flashes of fluorescent blue at significant times. The "lost in a daydream of blue" lyrics alerted me to the fact that this particular song would have spiritual significance to me.

So when Union Jack crossed over, and before Little Jack was born, the song from a Volvo commercial kept playing in my head. The song was "I Adore You" by Melpo Mene with the lyrics:

"Lost in a daydream of blue
And I feel so free
And then it's like I fall from the sky
Everything that I see is you
And you should know that I'm
Thinking about what you said
When you held my hand"
"Oh I adore you"

It was also particularly interesting that they gave me this song because during Union Jack's last days while he would be lying on his bed, I would pet him and hold his front paw telling him to be sure and come back to me. Even the part about "When you held my hand" also made sense. It was Union Jack telling me that he adored me and was coming back to me.

At one point, before Little Jack was born and after Union Jack had passed, Union Jack's vibes were so incredibly strong around me that I could feel him. I would even turn around to see if he was there. Of note, Union Jack's vibes stopped being around me when Little Jack was born, although I did not know he had reincarnated at that time.

All during March of 2008, I kept hearing Paul McCartney's song "Simply Having a Wonderful Christmas Time" which I thought was strange for that time of year. Why would I be hearing a Christmas song in March?

Then one morning towards the end of March, I had the urge to send some e-mails to a few Springer Spaniel breeders. I knew I was taking a shot in the dark but I felt compelled to do it anyhow. It was the same urge I had when I was guided to the classified ad for my Union Jack in the years before.

On March 31, I received an email from one of the breeders who said I should contact a local breeder named Jeri who just had a new litter born on March 30th.

It turned out the breeder's kennel name was "Yuletide Springers!" I later learned that my Union Jack's father and grandfather came from Jeri's Yuletide Springer bloodline. It was obvious to me that I was being "guided" and that was "why" I kept hearing McCartney's Christmas song.

When I pulled out Union Jack's Certificate of Pedigree, low and behold, all of his Yuletide Springer's ancestors were listed on it which added further confirmation.

All this was right in front of me and I never knew it until I was guided to this information. All those events really let me know spiritual guidance is real and the process of how your prayers are answered! Another interesting note about this Yuletide litter, there were 4 male pups. Only one of those pups had the same markings as my previous Union Jack and Jody Girl.

The other side had really made it easy for me to be guided to the right pup. Because of my incredible spiritual experiences with Union Jack and Jody Girl, I named my new Springer pup Union Jack II and call him Little Jack.

Because he was too young to come home yet, I would go visit Little Jack at Yuletide Springers. I kept hearing "Only Yesterday" by the Carpenters.

Here are some of the lyrics:
  "I have found my home here in your arms
  Nowhere else on earth I'd really rather be
  Life waits for us
  Share it with me
  The best is about to be
  So much is left for us to see"

All I could think about was when I was carrying Union Jack in my arms and kissing him. I know the lyric "I have found my home here in your arms" had something to do with Union Jack communicating to me about "the best is yet to be" as new Little Jack.

On May 27th, when Little Jack was eight weeks old, I brought him home. He immediately started playing with my other dog and was totally unconcerned about his new surroundings. It was like he had always been here!

For about three days, he did a lot of the same things that Big Jack did right before he passed. I call them carryovers which are really confirmations.

One night approximately six weeks after I brought Little Jack home, he was sleeping on the floor while I was on my computer. I looked down at my new sleeping pup and super imposed over his body was the image of Union Jack sitting up and looking directly at me for a few moments.

I KNEW that my Union Jack was confirming that he had, indeed, come back to me. This was no hallucination! It was the most vivid heartfelt confirmation I've ever experienced. It was as real as my breath. I knew what it was about and was so

Thankful to know that my Union Jack was back with me!

As you know, the eyes are the window of the soul and sometimes when I glance at Little Jack, it's like Union Jack is looking back at me. I can see it in his eyes. It sends chills down my spine. When people meet Little Jack for the first time, a lot of them remark how much he looks like Union Jack which I think is a subconscious response because, spiritually speaking, he really is my Union Jack.

I wanted to share my story since a lot of people don't understand or know what I have experienced. Juli the breeder told me pets are our guardian Angels. I know that to be true.

I truly believe this loving soul, who came to me as Jody Girl, and then Union Jack and now Little Jack are reincarnations.

All three of them were/are liver and white English Springer Spaniels and a part of my soul.

I call them my Three Angels.

My Three Angels
Jody Girl, Union Jack & Union Jack II

Pickles Reunites with Joanna

J Hogan, Coon Rapids, Mn.

My little Miniature Schnauzer Pickles died on Oct 6, 2008. Pickles was not just my pet. She was my companion having come into my life when I first became disabled and was filled with terrible pain, both physically and mentally.
I was so devastated with a terrible depression related to not only the loss of my physical capabilities, but the loss of my profession. Pickles was my "angel" and lifesaver.

In late Sept Pickles collapsed requiring me to take her to the Emergency Vet Services here. She seemed to improve from what appeared to be a "secondary" type of Immune Mediated Hemolytic Anemia and was sent home that same day on medication. Unfortunately, the next day she again collapsed and was again returned to the Emergency Vet. This time she wasn't improving and on Monday, the next day, was taken to the University of Minnesota Veterinary Hospital. She remained there a week to the day with every attempt made to save her life. That Monday she required <u>another</u> blood transfusion. The decison was made to stop the battle and allow her to cross over. It was the most terrible experience of my life, to hold her and watch her life just pass from her.

About three weeks passed and my grief was still overwhelming. My neighbor was actually concerned about my welfare and had come over with the "want ads" suggesting that I seriously look for another puppy.

Initially, I had no interest in finding another dog, but by afternoon my attitude had changed slightly and I decided to at least look at the ads. I checked the first ad and called the breeder. The voice was so familiar on the other end. Finally, I asked if he was related to the man I had bought Pickles from. Low and behold, it was the same breeder which I thought immediately was an "omen."

I went to look at his two little puppies. My immediate sense was to buy the "salt and pepper" female he had. Then, I started vacillating between the two. My thought was "oh this one looks more like Pickles...this one acts more like Pickles." Back and forth I went for almost two hours with those two puppies.

Suddenly, I realized that all I was doing was attempting to find a replacement for Pickles, or to actually "find her" again. I told the man that I was sorry, but that I guessed that I really wasn't ready for a dog yet. I was still looking for my Pickles.

I came home saddened and very disappointed! My grief intensified again. I told my husband that I was "never going to get another dog, this was just too painful." I had resigned myself to not getting another dog, ever again.

The weekend passed and it was now Monday. I was straightening up in the kitchen, cleaning up all the junk on the kitchen table when I was compelled to pick up those "want ads" again. As I picked it up, I had the strangest sense that I had to look at those listings again. Why? I haven't a clue.

I picked it up and went to the "dogs for sale page." I didn't go to the next listing down from the puppies I had actually gone to see, but went about half way down the page to a "Miniature Schnauzer Puppies for Sale" which was totally unrealistic as they were in Iowa.

This "compulsion" overwhelmed my sense of reality but I had to call the number. A very nice woman answered the phone. It happened to be that she was sitting at work by her computer when we started to talk. She had one female Schnauzer remaining, "Heide." She sent me a few pictures, but those pictures just didn't "trigger" any feeling of attachment at all. I told her that the puppy was cute, but that when I looked at the picture it just "didn't feel right." I told her that I guessed that I "just wasn't ready yet to get another puppy." I told her that I didn't even understand why I had called her.

On a second note, my daughter was going to be having twin girls in December which I shared with this woman and told her that I should probably just focus my attention on my two new little granddaughters when they were born. Even my daughter in her "feelings" of joy felt and just knew that "my Pickles would be coming home." Then Jamie told me that she was also pregnant and going to be having her child in May.

Out of the blue she began telling me that because of her own pregnancy she had also decided to breed her one year old female, Jorja. As soon as she told me this I felt this "sense, feeling" that I just couldn't understand. Then, she told me that Jorja had been bred on October 8th which was just two days after Pickles had passed.

I can't explain it, but I immediately had this "sense." I told Jodi, "You may think I am totally nuts, but I think my Pickles is going to come back to me." Jodi really didn't seem to react negatively to what I had said about Pickles coming back. I also said to her, "my Pickles had her right ear standing up. If one of those new puppies has her ear standing up that will really be the tip off."

Another weird coincidence about this upcoming second litter was that Pickles had also been born in December and I got her in February. With Jorja's pregnancy, her puppies would be born in December and the puppies would be ready to leave her in February. Hmmmmm.

Well, on December 11 those puppies were born. Miracles abounding in this litter!

First, a Miniature Schnauzer will usually only have four, or five puppies. Jorja had eight. Jamie sent me a picture of the litter about two days after they were born. I looked at that picture. There at the bottom of the picture was this tiny, light colored little bundle. I just knew that was Pickles.

I immediately wrote to Jamie and told her, "I want that little light puppy at the bottom of the picture." She immediately wrote back to me. That little light puppy was the "only" salt and pepper female in the litter. Now, that wasn't just the only coincidence.

When I got the individual pictures of each puppy there was my little salt and pepper female "with her left ear standing straight up.' Now, that may change as the ears fill in and grow, but I certainly took that as a "sign," a confirmation from something higher was letting me know that this was indeed my little Fickle!

Beside the upright ear there were two other confirmations for me. The puppy also had a dark streak down her entire back just as my little Pickles had.

Sweetest Baby Pickles

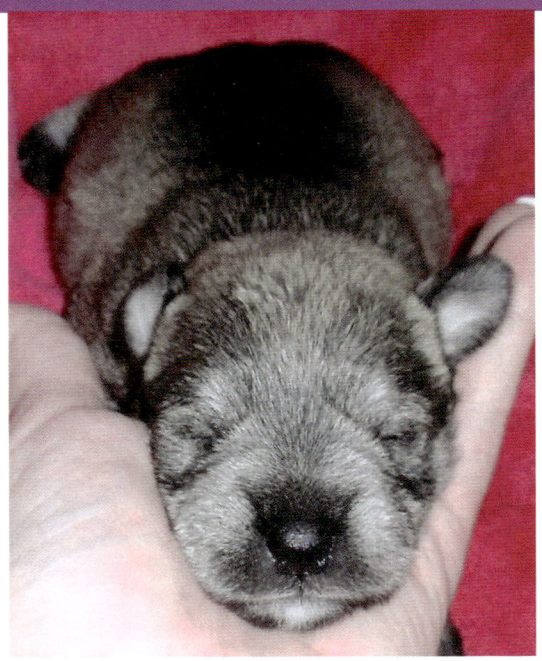

Also a white "heart" encircling her mouth, just the same as my Pickles.   Now, I am just two weeks away from picking up my Pickles. Three days ago I received another email with individual pictures of the puppies. I started to go thru the row of pictures. With each one I looked at I became a little sadder.

W th every puppy, I found myself thinking, "This one is nothing like Pickles. The stature is different. They have coarser fur, etc." I started to think to myself, "Maybe I am crazy, maybe this is all some delusion I have conjured up in my head to appease my own grief.

Finally, I got to the second to the last picture and looked. I became absolutely hysterical. I began sobbing uncontrollably and just screamed out loud, "My God, thank you. This is Pickles."   This little puppy was nothing like the rest. She was smaller framed, thinner "fly away" fur just like my little girl. It was as though I had received a picture of Pickles the day after I had gotten her.

I printed that picture out and handed it to my husband as soon as he walked in the door from work. "Ooohhh," he said. "a picture of Pickles when she was a puppy.

Where did you come across that?"

He was slightly amazed when I told him that was the "new Pickles." I think that my husband is finally starting to believe in "possibilities." Well, I will be getting my "little girl" in just under two weeks and I am continuing to "believe."

After reading Friend's story, I have a fantasy that my Pickles will be obviously excited to see me too. I have her bed ready, all her toys lined up for her. I am sending a picture of my Pickles along with the new puppy photos. I have always believed in miracles.

When Pickles was ill, I just couldn't believe that God had not answered my pleas to save her. God has never denied my heartfelt prayers and I just "didn't get why she didn't get better when she was so sick."

I 'm glad you had your web site www.JustPlainLovebooks.com. I just knew I wasn't crazy and KNEW I could not be the only person that either felt this way, or had this type of thing happen.

I am hoping that I will have additional confirmations tomorrow when I bring my "new Pickles" home. I did have a chance to talk to her on the phone a few days ago. The breeder Jamie put her up to the phone. I started to call her and say, "Pickles, my little Picky, how's my girl, this is mama..." Jamie said, "Wow, how strange. Pickles immediately started licking the phone like a little crazy girl."

Then, she put her back down on the floor and she immediately started to cry as loudly as if she was "injured." Well, all I could do was cry. I told Jodi, "of course she licked the phone, she knew it was her mama." I think when she gets home tomorrow there will be many "awakenings" occurring.

I choose to believe that God is answering my prayers, I am getting my miracle - it is just not the miracle I prayed for, I'm getting my "Pickles back!

Pickles (II). Today I picked her up. I had to drive a bit, almost two hours. Colleen went with me which would allow me to carry Pickles on the trip back. All the way to Mankato I shared the "peculiar" circumstances involving my coming to find and now picking up Pickles. I assure you Colleen was a "skeptic" and stated so. She did share that she wished she could believe in such "miraculous" occurrences and that if I believed this to be Pickles "reincarnation" she was most happy for me.

Jamie, the breeder pulled right up next to us in the parking lot. Colleen was the first to see little Pickles and all she could say was, "Oh my God, is she cute... she is just something. Joanna you're gonna die when you see her."

It was cold so we got out of my car and went to sit in the back seat of Jami's car. Suddenly there was my little Pickles peeping at us and she was a sight! It was like looking back almost nine years to see my "first" Pickles as a puppy. Jami's mom handed her to me. I had expected her to be somewhat reluctant and fearful of a new person in her life. Not a bit!

She immediately literally starred at my face with a fixed gaze. Then, she just melted in my arms and placed her head on my arm, totally relaxed. She laid there for a couple minutes and then crawled upward laying her head on my shoulder and again immediately relaxed almost going to sleep. She kept turning her head to stare in to my face. I tend to be a somewhat emotional person and the tears just started to flow. I looked at everyone present in the car and just said, "This is Pickles, I just feel it."

Then, thinking out loud I said, "This is the exact position when I lost her, and now it's the way she comes back to me." When I put her to sleep she was laying in my arms with her little head on my shoulder. I covered her head with her blanket reassuring her that everything would be ok and that I loved her." I nodded to the veterinarian simply saying, "It's OK." She totally went limp in my arms and I knew she was gone.

Now, she was lying on my shoulder, just the same way as when I had lost her. Again, I just could do nothing, but cry and thank God. I can't tell you how many times on the way home Colleen would say, "Joanna, it's like she knows you!" Pickles slept almost the entire way home except for the several times she tried to jump into the back seat.

Of note: my first Pickles "hated" to sit in the front seat and no matter how I would attempt to keep her there, she would always jump into the back seat.

When we arrived home my other neighbor Sue, came over to see our new Pickles. She picked her up and immediately Pickles looked her square in the eye and licked her face. Now, it would seem to me that normally a "new puppy" would have some sort of "stranger anxiety." Never once did I notice any anxiety, or fear with meeting me, Colleen and now Sue. The first thing that came out of Sue's mouth was, "She looks just like Pickles."

I then took Pickles into the house and up the stairs to the living room. She immediately walked down the hall, peeked in at my bedroom, looked back and forth as if to say, "Yup, all the same-still here." She then came back down the hall and sat right at the top of the stairs looking down in just the exact manner that my first Pickles had done for years.

I couldn't wait to show her to my sister Tonie who is nearly 86. I put Pickles on her lap and she immediately faced Toni and started to lick her face as if a joyful reunion. This once rambunctious little puppy was now content to lie on Toni's lap all evening. Not a peep or any anxiety you would expect from an eight week old puppy just separated from the only owners it had known.

Also, Pickles had a small bed in the kitchen where she would always be if I were working there. This Pickles was "immediately" drawn to that bed and lays in it displaying all the "old" positions she would assume in her first life. i.e. "head out the front on the floor," "upside down with her head over the arm," "curled up in a ball on the 'right' side." These little nuances are all too familiar for a "new little puppy" who is supposedly just "learning."

Here's one last little "ditty" about new Pickles. My old Pickles would never eat in the kitchen. She would sit by the kitchen counter and just wait for preparation of supper to be completed.

Suddenly, last week "new" little Pickles started to
sit by the counter just below the sink as I was getting supper
ready. I was cutting up some food on a plate for my sister.
Pickles started barking and jumping uncontrollably. Finally, I
took a paper plate and
cut a few pieces of roast beef on that plate.

When I set it down in front of her, Pickles immediately picked
up that paper plate and took it to the dining room, just in front
of the patio doors and then ate. This was the <u>exact</u> "spot" o d
Pickles would eat her supper. After she finished the meat or the
plate, she again picked it up and started carrying around the
empty plate just like old Pickles would do too. I just love all of
these continuing confirmations that my Pickles is home!

After today, I could never doubt that a miracle has occurred
in our lives. God with all his might has given me the gift of
uniting me with one of the strongest love's I have ever felt in
my life. I feel wonderful, as if this hole in my heart has been
healed. I will continue to "update" you of any new happenings
in the life of my little Pickles.

Boco Returns as Baj
Then Reincarnates Again as Rocky
Maili

This is a story about a wonderful, beautiful, large and very macho black lab that had charisma like his owner Steve. Steve was a California fireman, a surfer and known throughout the beach community as social, friendly and gregarious. Steve had met Boco on the beach boardwalk on earlier occasions while he was being walked by his owner. Boco and Steve shared a mutual admiration for each other (and there was this pang of "I wish you were mine, and I want you to live with me" kind-of intuitive message going on.)

When Boco was 6 months old, the owner knocked on Steve's door. She asked 'will you take my dog? I can not keep him in my apartment. You obviously belong to each other." Tears were running down her cheeks, "I can't keep him, my landlord won't let me have him,----- please..... Be good to him, and have a wonderful long life together."

Steve looked into Boco's eyes, and Boco looked into Steve's, and they both knew that they were a team. Happiness and contentment flooded their macho chests. When Boco was 17, he went out of the gate that surrounded their cottage, and was fatally hit by a truck.

When a neighbor told Steve what had happened, he vowed he would never be able to replace such a friend, and he wasn't even going to try. The next morning, without Boco to start his day, Steve was empty. He went through the motions, but there was no joy.   Life and his "home" as he knew it was gone. He began to build a new life but there was always something missing.

About 9 mos. later a young woman came to Steve's door, holding a leash with an adorable Rhodesian ridgeback puppy bouncing on the other end. She gave Steve that look that was familiar --, with the words "can you please take my dog? Please take my dog, and give him a good home."

Steve named the puppy Baj. Baj had seen Steve a few times at the boardwalk and would become exuberant whenever they would encounter one another.

The young woman felt as if she was "keeping a pre-destined relationship from flowering". She said..."I know he prefers you to me. If I really love him, I have to give him to you."

Steve had vowed that he would not get attached to another dog again, but some things are "out of our control."

Four years later, I met Steve who became my boyfriend. When it became very clear that Baj was definitely going to be a part of our relationship, I insisted that I meet his dog.

I had them both over for dinner. My children and I instantly became charmed by and enamored with Baj. Even on our first meeting it was so natural to have him around. Baj began to spend nights with us and we would include him in our activities. My children would refer to him as their dog.

When Steve would go on long trips, Baj would stay with us and slept next to me. We had an understanding that we wanted "to keep each other." Finally one day Steve came over and acknowledged the look Baj had in his eyes when Steve said, "okay Baj, let's go home".

Baj looked at me, looked at Steve, looked at my sons and daughter, and walked back towards the bed we had made for him, laid down, and looked at Steve as if to say "can we talk about this tomorrow?"

Steve said, "Well, Baj, I guess you are making it really clear. I think you like it with them better, and I can't say I blame you pal. You have two cats, three kids, all those hugs, walks, you get to sleep in a real human bed every night, take daily rides in the car, beach trips whenever you ask....." With tears in his eyes Steve said, "Maili, he's yours" although in my heart I already knew he was mine. We had connected on a heart and soul level many months before, we just couldn't tell Steve.

Baj got sick with leukemia at the early age of 7. He became weaker and weaker. I took him to the beach the last day, and lifted his weak body out of the back seat, and knew for sure he would never get to go to the shore again. The next day he died, after waiting for the whole family to finish their day.

He took his last breath after each of us had told him
what he had meant to us. We cried so hard,
and couldn't imagine a day with out Baj.
Shortly after Baj's passing Steve and I broke up.

Because Baj was the only dog that I had ever had,
I didn't know what to do. I was so empty without him, and I
would wander from room to room expecting that I would see
him. I wanted Baj back.
My daughter wanted me to be open to adopting a puppy, and
not necessarily a Rhodesian ridgeback.

In April, about 5 months after saying good-bye to Baj,
my daughter called and said "Mom come with me,
have an open mind, and let's look at these baby Labradors
that are advertised in the local newspaper.

Reluctantly, I went. We looked, and I saw this adorable little
black "runt of the litter"---very shy but with a glance that said'
--"I know you, don't you know me?"

I went home, convinced that I was to wait for a Rhodesian
ridgeback. I had dreams about the little black guy,
at least three times.
Finally after three weeks of utter confusion, I called the owner,
and asked if there were any black labs left. He said only one.
If you want him you better come and get him.

So, I did. My son John named him Rocky. The first time we brought him in the house, he went laid and down in the very spot where Baj had taken his last breath and then looked at us as if to say "yes, I am back, and this is my home."
The house felt normal again.

When Rocky was three months old I took him for a walk in Torrey Pines State Park where I would often go to meditate with Baj, and where I buried Baj's ashes.
When Rocky and I got to the entrance of the park,
Rocky took off running as fast as he could.

When I caught up with him, he had started to dig up Baj's ashes. Rocky turned and looked at me with such an intense stare --as if to say "now do you know who I am?"
I smiled, and knew I had come to know and understand one of the best secrets on the planet. Animal souls do reincarnate. Rocky is now 11 years young and so passionately loved. He is my constant loving buddy, and the center of my heart.

Rocky's favorite Cat: Maui Reincarnates as Kaipo (Baby)
Maili

In a round cage with several other kittens prominently displayed in the middle of a La Jolla pet store, this six week old black long-haired fluff with gorgeous eyes was very deliberately vying for my attention. Although I already had two other cats at home, once we looked at each other, he owned me!
I had only gone to buy cat food yet had no other choice than to also bring home a lot of fur that had a kitten somewhere inside. The boys named him Maui and he immediately fit right in.

Every night and as soon as the bedroom light went out, Maui would get up on the bed, pull back the covers and tap my cheek with his paw. Slowly but surely he taught me that his gesture was my cue to place my hand near my cheek. Once situated, he would sleep all night long with the palm of my hand as his pillow. It became our special nightly ritual!

During the day he was my shadow, following me everywhere. When I would leave and come back he would greet me and have kitty conversation with me. He'd ask me why I left and where I went, and of course we also had to discuss all of his activities. Soon after, he would settle down into our normal routine.

If I was away for several days on end, I didn't hear the end of it for days!!! Can a cat actually meow THAT much for THAT long? How I wish I knew exactly what he was saying, then maybe it was best that I didn't.

At 17 Maui began experiencing heart problems. He threw a blood clot that led to paralysis in his right front foot. That seemed to clear up fine. Two weeks later he developed another clot in his back left foot which eventually silently created gangrene in the area that was unable to have normal blood flow.

The day I discovered the gangrene I looked into his eyes, knowing there was no hope or resolution, and said "as much as I love you and want you to stay, I have to help you through this." I made an appointment that same day to help him cross the Rainbow Bridge.

One hour before his appointment he came into my room inherently knowing we needed to say our goodbyes to one another. He stretched out in front of me and soulfully looked into my eyes. As I clutched him to my heart while carefully holding and tenderly embracing him in my arms I said heart stated

"I love you so much and this is the hardest thing for me to do. This is not something you can recover from. I want you to come find me again as my kitty." I tearfully and with a prayer in my heart said "Maui find a way to come back to me, because Rocky did it and I know you can do it too!"

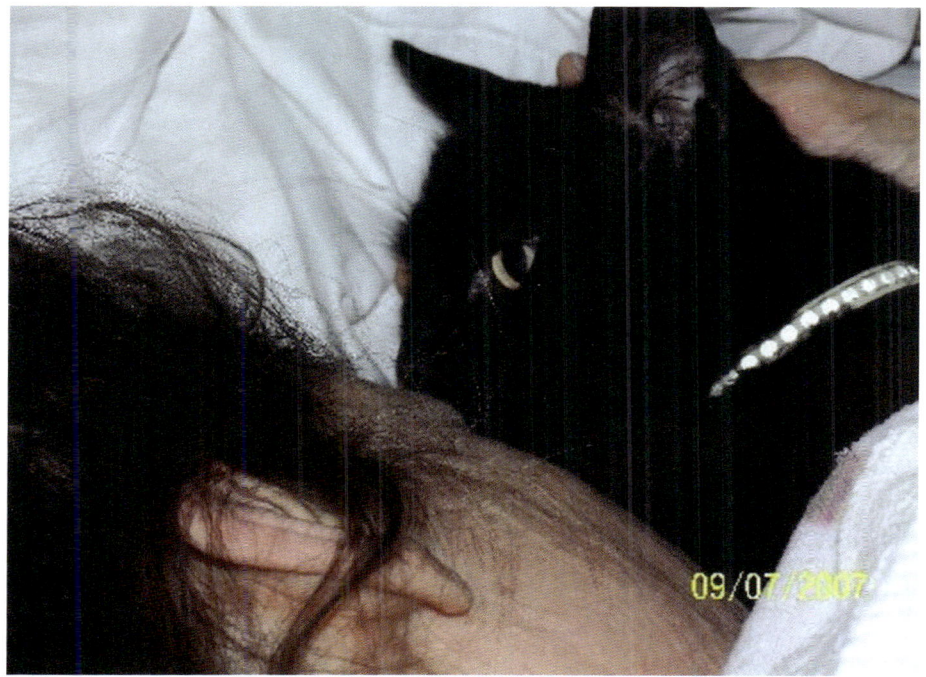

Before we left home, I snipped some of Maui's fur for a memento and slipped his collar off and put it all into an envelope. Rocky (whose story preceded this) was in the other room intently listening to our conversation.

We all, even Rocky, went to the vet as a family. We all were in the room where Maui was to be released from his earthly suffering.

I held my beautiful, precious 17 year fur friend in my arms while the vet gave him an injection to relax him saying "I will be back in 10 minutes and you can spend some time with him."

Rocky kissed him first and as I was kissing Maui he collapsed. Rocky saw him fall lifeless in my arms and immediately put his head down on his own paws, as if to honor and pay homage to his buddy. Maui had passed without needing the final injection.

My home was empty. Rocky and I were both terribly depressed.

After three weeks, I decided to get another kitty to cheer us up. Frankie a beautiful Maine coon cat became the newest member of our household. He absolutely adored Rocky, kissed him on the lips and helped ease our sadness.

Although everyone loved Frankie, that soul connection was not there with either of us.

154

Seven months later, browsing through the Sunday newspaper, I came across an advertisement for four weeks old kittens. I figured why not call as I had nothing else to do that day and the owners said come right over if you'd like to see them.

By the time I go there only a pale Balinese colored male with beautiful blue eyes was left. I had no intention of doing anything but entertaining myself with precious precocious kittens that afternoon.

The owner held that kitty up for me to look at and the kitty looked straight into my eyes with that soft stare of recognition that my soul understood. Once again, I was taking home an unplanned feline that my heart knew was meant to be mine. He rode home on my shoulder purring the whole time.

The moment he walked through our door, the house felt normal again, it felt like home! He immediately adapted to everything and strolled through the house fearlessly as if he had been there before.

Unexplainably all the sadness and hurt in my heart just disappeared, as if we all were a complete family again. The unsettledness in the household was resolved.

I then contacted an animal communicator to hopefully validate what Rocky and I already knew in our hearts.
She confirmed my hearts knowing that Maui was home again.

His name is Kaipo, which means sweetheart in Hawaiian. He immediately started to sleep with his head in my palm just as he did when he was Maui and knew where to eat. He loves Rocky and runs up to him and puts his nose on Rocky's nose.

He seemed to know all the landmarks of his previous life, like where the cat door was and how to use it. When I showed him his former collar he grabbed it and rolled on it and looked at me as if to say this is mine.

It's wonderful to be a family again!

*Be sure to read our other wonderful
Just Plain Love® reincarnation stories*

"I'm Home!" a Cat's Never Ending Love Story
"I'm Home!" A Horse's Never Ending Love Story

We invite you to submit yours!

Brent's motto:
"*I want my books and art to DO good as* well as BE good!"

As a pet reincarnation expert, Brent and Friend's international travels for workshops, seminars and speaking tours inspire hope, educate and expand awareness and prove that prayers are answered and pet reincarnation is real!

Brent Atwater helps change lives in addition to inspiring hope by providing you and your pet tools, techniques and solutions that enable you and your animal companions to communicate, facilitate healing and to have a better quality of life.

Brent Atwater's medical intuitive diagnostic work with a global clientele of people and pets has documented, published and respected case results. She collaborates with and participates in ongoing holistic integrative energy medicine and the science of medical intuition diagnostic research and independent case studies with the world's leading researchers.

Her work establishes evidence based research that creates and documents the bridging of traditional and alternative healthcare.

Brent, a pioneer in healing art medicine scientifically documented the healing energy, diagnostic abilities and healing benefits of her art for health and healing Paintings That Heal® (www.BrentAtwater.com). She is one of the contemporary American painters who are bringing forth a new cultural renaissance by blending her classical artistic training with spirituality and energy infused into her healing art.

Ms. Atwater's Just Plain Love® Books, weekly radio shows, podcasts, blogs, invigorating and inspiring audience participatory workshops (with awesome demonstrations), upbeat healthcare seminars, speaking tours, fundraising contributions, book signings and consultations contribute to bringing transformative and positive results to benefit the lives of others.

Visit her Website:
www.BrentAtwater.com.

The Just Plain Love® Story

"Experiencing pediatric intensive care, oncology, burn or trauma units to me, is a heart wrenching jolt to anyone's world. I had to summon all my "heart" to handle the various states of disrupted life. Right then and there I decided that a positive Light needed to shine on these struggling souls, so new to earth and so old to disease and ravaged by procedures and treatments.

I decided that I was going to find a way to offer an uplifting spin on health negatives and to create a door of communication, a treasure of heartwarming and reassuring perspectives to those "hands off" health subjects.

It is my intent to provoke a muffled laugh, instigate a tiny smile, mischievous giggle or just an environmental change and safe place for a brief moment that would add a sparkle to a weary eye.

AND I am going to give a comforting and supportive symbolic "hug" to each patient and reader by filling them with a sense of pride in themselves for having endured their own health battle by providing a tangible 'Badge of Honor' souvenir as a permanent way to celebrate their courage!

I was unable to have children, so this is my way of giving back. **In 1987 the Just Plain Love® Charitable Trust was born.**"

Brent Atwater's Other Dream:

Just Plain Love® Plays, Performances & Educational Programs for Children with "Poof" the Angel & "Friend" the companion angel therapy dog

Surely, Ms Atwater dreams, there can be participatory mini skits/plays held in healthcare and medical facilities lasting about 5 to 15 minutes that would hold a patient's attention, entertain, educate, rehabilitate and provide a few safe moments of mental relief through laughter, plus providing each patient with a tangible Badge of Honor to reward and recognize their courage.

For the past 20+ years Ms Atwater has researched, tested, rewritten and reworked each children's healing book and play according to the storytelling responses and reactions from healthy and unhealthy readers, caregivers, family, friends, medical and healthcare professionals, clients and her storytelling audience.

Ms Atwater's dream is to inspire the creative imagination of readers of all ages to replace negative thoughts about health issues, medical experiences, rehabilitative therapy and reentry into society with a positive "spin" on their journey to health and well being.

We hope you enjoyed this
Just Plain Love® Book.

If you would like information about Just Plain Love® Books, Kindle, Audio or eBooks, or other information please contact:

Brent@BrentAtwater.com

Friend is available

for paw signings
guest appearances
fundraising & hugs!

As are some of the
other wonderful
reincarnated dogs that
have shared their
stories with you!

Contact:
Brent Atwater

Join Friend's
MySpace and Facebook groups for more pet reincarnation stories
and to share yours!
http://groups.myspace.com/petreincarnation
http://www.facebook.com/group.php?gid=59877299590

**Become a fan of Friend Atwater's Official Facebook Site
for** "I'm Home!" a Dog's Never Ending Love Story

**Visit Friend's
Facebook , Twitter , YouTube, Tumblr and MySpace**
www.myspace.com/Friend Atwater
http://www.youtube.com/user/FriendAtwater
http://www.facebook.com/people/Friend-Atwater/1611111869
http://twitter.com/FriendImHome

Subscribe to our Blogs:
http://justplainlovechildrensbooks.blogspot.com/
http://petreincarnation.blogspot.com/
http://holisticpetmedicalalternativehealing.blogspot.com/

Just Plain Love® Books

inspiring smiles, hugs and healing for every reader's heart!
www.JustPlainLoveBooks.com

Other Just Plain Love® Titles, Kindle & Audio Books
Children's Books:
Cancer Kids—God's Special Children
Cancer and MY Daddy!

Health Books:
Medical Intuitive Diagnosis – Medical Intuitive Diagnostic Imaging™
Learn to Access & Interpret the Energy language *of Medical Disorders, Disease & Health Issues*

Healing Yourself! 23 Ways to Heal Diseases, Disorders Medical Conditions and Health Issues

Animal Lovers' Books:
"The Dog with a "B" on His Bottom!"
"I'm Home!" a Dog's Never Ending Love Story
"I'm Home!" a Cat's Never Ending Love Story
"I'm Home!" a Horse's Never Ending Love Story

Visit Brent Atwater's websites:
www.BrentAtwater.com
www.JustPlainLoveBooks.com
www.BrentEnergyWork.com

Visit Brent Atwater's and Friend Atwater's
Facebook, MySpace, YouTube, Tumbler and Twitter pages!

"I'm Home!" A Dog's Never Ending Love Story
1st Printing 2010

6862412R0

Made in the USA
Lexington, KY
02 October 2010